Self-regulation in Everyday Life

A How-to Guide for Parents

Dr. Heather MacKenzie

Wired Fox Publications

St. Catharines, Ontario, Canada

First published in 2015

by Wired Fox Publications

St. Catharines, Ontario, Canada

wiredfoxpublications@gmail.com

Illustrations by Amy Preveza

Library and Archives of Canada Cataloguing in Publication

Self-regulation in Everyday Life

Heather MacKenzie

Includes bibliographical references and index

ISBN 978-0-9684466-8-3

Table of Contents

Acknowledgements

I want to thank all of the reviewers of this book who provided thoughtful reviews and helpful feedback as well as encouragement. They gave their time, knowledge and expertise so generously. I am greatly indebted to Susan Deike, Joselynne Jaques, Randee Loucks, Dana Lust, Sheila Mansell, Elizabeth Matthews, Kirsten Ness, Tamara Tate, and Allison Waks. I am also indebted to Teeya Scholten and Johanna Brown for their feedback on earlier versions.

Susan made Grice happy by helping me 'avoid prolixity' – one of the Gricean principles. Joselynne shared her experience in working with parents and in using the spark* model. Randee helped immeasurably in prompting me to make the format more coherent. Dana provided excellent feedback on the need to help tie self-regulation and executive functions into the reality of eight-year-olds. Sheila provided that extra 'push' to add illustrations of implementation. Elizabeth and Tamar both receive my editorial 'eagle eyes' award – thank you for finding all the glitches in the text. Kirsten allowed me to draw from her experience and knowledge. Allison, you always make me think in ways I hadn't anticipated – for that, I sincerely thank you.

Thanks goes to the wonderfully creative Amy Preveza for making the concepts come alive with her illustrations throughout and on the cover.

Heartfelt thanks go to my husband, Bill, for his unconditional support and editorial comments throughout this process.

Preface

More and more we're recognizing that children need help learning how and when to control their bodies, thinking, and emotions. Some children learn these things readily but others need some direct teaching.

I'm sure you recognize the antsy little people in your child's group of friends. You know the ones who're a little louder and perhaps more accident-prone than the others.

I was one of them. I was constantly gouging and scraping knees and elbows. I didn't look before I leaped. I was quiet and shy around strangers but rather loud and raucous at home or among friends. I used to put on my recording of the Swedish Rhapsody and dash around the room, moving with the music. It seemed that I only had high gear. Along with little self-regulation, I had a wild imagination. I recall pretending to 'deep-sea dive' off a couch, breaking my collar bone in the process.

Photo of a happier me outside and setting my own agenda.

Not only was my body busy, so was my brain. I jumped into things with partial information. If someone's explanation went on too long, my mind drifted. This meant that I tried to do things with only part of the information I needed. As you can imagine, I got negative reactions from many people. I went to kindergarten at a convent school. I recall the nuns taking me for walks and showing me "what the good girls did". I thoroughly enjoyed the chances to tour the school and escape my classroom. The nun's message, however, was lost on me.

I cried through most of Grade 1. I already knew a lot of what they were teaching and found the strict rules difficult to deal with. I couldn't go to the toilet when I needed or wanted to, I had to wait for certain times or put up my hand and ask. I guess it just felt very oppressive (and boring) to me, as it does to many other children today.

School didn't really improve a whole lot until my Master's degree program. By that point (my early 20s), I'd figured out how I learn best and how to self-regulate a little better.

Learning to self-regulate has been a long, slow process for me. I want to help other children learn sooner so they have a more positive experience in school. My work with children with special needs has shown that children can learn to control their bodies, thinking, and emotions. They just need to be taught in positive, fun ways.

This book is for every parent who wants to help their child be better prepared for school and for life in general. Parents are naturals for playfully engaging their children. There are many small opportunities every day to sneak in short, enjoyable practice-sessions in the car, bus or train, in the line-up at the grocery store, at the dinner table, at bedtime, or just about any other time. Even if you're busy, take that moment to engage your child in learning self-regulation. Put down that phone or other electronic device and have fun with your child. You'll see the benefits.

This guide is to help parents of children, two to eight years of age, enhance their self-regulation in everyday situations. This guide will explain how to practice and extend body, cognitive and emotional self-regulation using activities that occur in regular family life. The goal is to avoid 'special' practice sessions. We don't need to add more to your already busy calendars.

In the chapters ahead, you'll learn to help your child regulate his own body, brain, and feelings.

In the first chapter, we discuss self-regulation, what it is, why it's important, and whether your child needs help.

In the next chapter, we look at how self-regulation is approached using the **spark*** model[1]. **spark*** stands for *Self-regulation Program of Awareness and Resilience in Kids.*

Then, we review some factors that are critical to your success in learning self-regulation. These include making sure your child is in an appropriate mood to work on self-regulation, how to make practicing fun, and how to keep your child thinking and learning.

The next three chapters are your guides for working on body, cognitive, and emotional self-regulation with your child.

In the last chapter are some key reminders for working on self-regulation.

Please note: The masculine pronoun will be used throughout this book for the sake of simplicity only.

When you get this book, you'll have access to many helpful resources and materials. We've found that, to keep the information current, it's best to put the resources on a website. That way, we can update and add to the resources and you can access them at any time. Simply email us at self.reg.everyday@gmail.com to get the password.

Resource and material files you'll find are:

ILLUSTRATIONS	Major features for describing objects
	Major parts of Well-structured stories
	Stop and Go signs
	Turtle Breathing
	Yoga positions
MATERIAL	Likes & Dislikes survey
	Household tasks
	Executive Function Survey
	Language of spark* cue cards
	Designing a yoga program
	Games for practicing self-regulation
	Selected songs and rhymes for Body self-regulation
RESOURCES**	Commercially available apps, books and materials
	Internet sites coordinated with activities
	Storybooks coordinated with target areas
TEMPLATE	Happy Thoughts bubble
	Shield

** We'll update these resources on a consistent basis so you don't run into outdated websites. Also, you'll find new resources we've added.

1 Self-regulation

What is self-regulation?

Self-regulation is the ability to consciously control your body, thinking, and emotions in ways appropriate for different situations. In learning to self-regulate, your child will learn to adjust the speed at which his body moves and where and when he should move it in different ways. For example, if your child is in a place of worship, he learns to use a quiet voice and not run. He learns that handsprings and yelling are for the playground and not inside the house. Learning self-regulation helps your child know when he needs to listen carefully and check that he understands what's being said. Self-regulation will also help him understand and respond appropriately to different emotions and feelings in himself and others.

What self-regulation is not

Learning self-regulation is completely different from your typical approaches to changing behavior in children. Usually, you wait for your child to misbehave (you might even warn him beforehand about what not to do), then you reprimand him when he does. You may penalize him by giving him a time-out or by losing some privilege, hoping he's learned from the experience.

With self-regulation, you teach your child before anything happens. You make sure he knows how to modulate and control his behavior, thinking and emotions in different situations. You help him understand what he needs to do, why and when. You increasingly give up control so he can be more independent. Ultimately, you can put your parental eagle eyes away and assume the role of coach and cheerleader to your child.

Self-regulation and executive functions

In developing self-regulation, your child will learn to consciously control something called his executive functions. Executive functions are brain circuits that help him organize his world, set priorities and put his ideas and thoughts together. Executive functions are located in the frontal lobes of our brains, just behind the fore-head (see the diagram to the right). Executive functions help us put our thoughts and ideas into action.

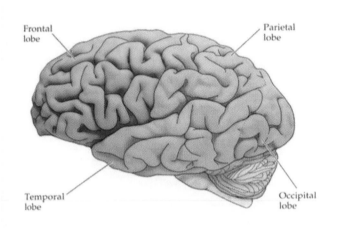

To get a clearer idea of how executive functions help us, imagine drawing the clown shown to the left. You need to:

- Plan and organize materials needed. Then decide how to approach the task. What I should draw first?

    • Stick with that plan and don't dive impulsively into drawing his fuzzy hair before drawing the main circle for his head.

    • Keep the image of the clown in mind while working, remembering that there are three pink circles on his mouth, for example.

- Check your work to make sure all the right parts are in the right place and look like the model.

- Be flexible when needed because plans may have to be adjusted if they're not working out.

2

The things I had to consider in that example are the key executive functions your child needs in day-to-day life. Here are the five key executive functions he'll practice in this program:

1. **Planning and organization** are involved from the instant your child decides to do something. He needs to think about what he intends to do and make a plan so he can finish the task completely and on time. If your child wants to build a marble run, he needs to find the pieces he wants as well as the marbles. *Planning and organization are the day-planners or organizers among the executive functions that help him stay directed and on task.*

2. **Inhibitory control** lets him direct his attention and actions even if there are temptations and distractions. Inhibitory control helps him ignore things that might interfere with what he's doing. It also helps him stop doing something if it isn't effective or appropriate. In addition, it keeps him persevering

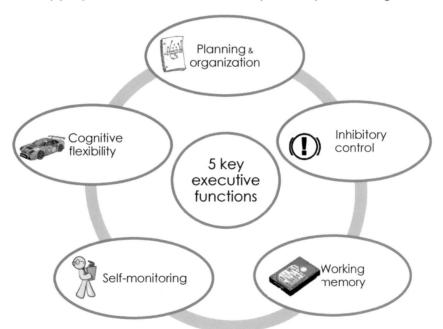

with a task even if it's difficult. For example, your child is printing; he may want to just get it done any old way because he's getting tired or his friends are playing; his inhibitory control helps him continue doing his best work until it's done. *Inhibitory control is the set of brakes among the executive functions that helps him star and stop when needed.*

3. **Working memory** lets your child keep ideas in his mind while putting them together in a complete picture. Working memory makes it possible to remember instructions, consider alternatives, multi-task and connect the 'right now' with future possibilities and/or past experiences. If you ask your child to tidy up his room and carry his dirty clothes to the laundry basket, he has to keep those instructions active in his working memory as he completes each part. *Working memory is the central processing unit of the executive functions.*

4. **Self-monitoring** is the supervisor or boss of the executive functions. It helps your child check his actions and thoughts to make sure he's heading in a direction he wants. If he needs to meet a goal and get his work done, he has to keep checking how he's doing and whether he's making headway. When your child brushes his teeth, he needs to make sure he brushes each tooth on both sides. He has to keep track of what he's done and where else he needs to brush so he doesn't forget anything.

5. **Cognitive flexibility** lets your child switch the way he's thinking or acting in response to changing cues and situations. If your child decides to wear a particular shirt but he finds it's in the laundry, he can change his whole outfit, pick a different shirt or ask to have his special shirt washed. *Cognitive flexibility is like self-righting car of executive functions; if it runs into a roadblock, it can flip around and keep going.*

Separating executive functions into five key ones is a bit artificial. All are intertwined and interdependent that it's really not easy to separate one from the other. Often when you're working on one executive function, you're also influencing one or more other functions. This means that, when we're working on self-regulation, we're helping your child take control of each of these executive functions.

What can improved self-regulation do?

When children improve their self-regulation, they can adjust their behavior, thinking, and emotions in relation to the demands of each situation. They can stay calm in exciting or stressful situations. They can make plans and follow them, as well as make changes if necessary. They can also wait for payoffs and take greater pleasure in their achievements.

Research shows that children with stronger self-regulation tend to have:

- Better mental health, greater feelings of happiness[2,3], and experience less anxiety and tension[4]

- Advanced social skills[5] and more resistance to persuasion (such as peer pressure)[6]

- More intrinsic motivation (that is, doing something for the pleasure or challenge) with less reliance on rewards for working[7]

- More interest and enjoyment in learning[8,9,10,11]

- Greater persistence[12] [13,14,15,16,17]

- More independence[18]

Self-regulation is central to becoming an independent, happy child and adult. Through it, your child learns to make decisions and to regulate his behavior, thinking, and emotions in all situations – at home, at school, in the community.

Does my child need work on self-regulation?

Do you find that you have to remind your child over and over and over to:

- ✓ Put his things away (like his jacket or toys)
- ✓ Calm down
- ✓ Slow down

✓ Use a quiet voice or speak a little louder

✓ Listen carefully

✓ Not hit or push other children

✓ Do something on his own from beginning to end (like homework or chores)

If you answered 'yes' to any of these questions, your child could benefit from working on self-regulation.

Look a little more thoroughly at your child's key executive functions by completing the *Executive Function Survey* on the next two pages. The survey isn't exhaustive but it will give you an idea how your child is self-regulating in everyday life. Often we get used to patterns of behavior and don't really notice if a child is different from others his age. Have a look at the age-appropriate household tasks (pages 72-73) to gain more perspective on what others do in your child's age group. The *Executive Function Survey* will help you summarize your day-to-day experience and let you look at some of these patterns. Go ahead and complete the survey.

You can find extra copies of the Executive Function Survey on the Self-regulation Everyday website (www.self-reg-everyday.com).

Now, let's look at your responses to the *Executive Function Survey*.

- <u>If you checked three or more items as occurring "very frequently" or "always"</u>, your child needs to improve his body, cognitive and emotional self-regulation.

- <u>If you checked six or more items as occurring "occasionally"</u>, there is room for improvement in self-regulation so your child would benefit from completing this program.

EXECUTIVE FUNCTION SURVEY

Please put a check (✓) in the column that tells how often you've seen your child behave in the way described by the sentence as <u>compared to other children his/her age.</u>

Child's name:	Today's date:

Person completing survey:	Relation to child:

Compared to other children my child's age, s/he …	Never	Rarely	Occasionally	Very frequently	Always	Don't know
PLANNING & ORGANIZING						
1. Gets stuck on parts of tasks and can't move forward.						
2. Becomes overwhelmed by too many options or large tasks.						
3. Needs to be told to start a task even when interested in doing it.						
4. Leaves his belongings messy and disorganized.						
5. Has trouble figuring out where to start an activity or task.						
INHIBITORY CONTROL						
1. Fails to stop himself from doing unsafe or inappropriate things (like running into the street, grabbing something from another person).						
2. Has difficulty managing worry or disappointment.						
3. Is easily distracted by noises, activity, sights, other people.						
4. Has difficulty delaying rewards or events.						
5. Gives up easily.						

Compared to other children my child's age, s/he ...	Never	Rarely	Occasionally	Very frequently	Always	Don't know
WORKING MEMORY						
1. Only remembers one thing when given tasks.						
2. Forgets what he is supposed to get when sent to fetch something.						
3. Becomes overwhelmed by too much information.						
4. Has difficulty retelling or re-enacting stories or events.						
5. Doesn't remember the names of other children.						
SELF-MONITORING						
1. Does not check for mistakes in his work or activities.						
2. Makes careless errors.						
3. Is unaware of how his behavior affects or impacts other people.						
4. Does not check his progress when doing a task or activity.						
5. Does not check back to the goal of a task to refresh his memory.						
COGNITIVE FLEXIBILITY						
1. Tries the same approach to a problem again and again even when it doesn't work.						
2. Is upset by new situations, people or activities.						
3. Resists change in plans, routines, food, clothes, etc.						
4. Locks in on a topic or activity and sticks with it even after others have moved on.						
5. Has difficulty making smooth transitions from activity to activity or place to place.						

Keep a copy of your responses on the *Executive Function Survey* so you can compare them after you've worked with your child for a few months.

ILLUSTRATION – seven year old boy (Jack)

Jack is a seven year old boy. His mom completed the Executive Function Survey. Here are the results:

EXECUTIVE FUNCTION SURVEY

Please put a check (✓) in the column that tells how often you've seen your child behave in the way described by the sentence as <u>compared to other children his/her age</u>.

Child's name: Jack · · · · · Today's date: 6/2/15

Person completing survey: Robbie · · · · Relation to child: Mom

Compared to other children my child's age, s/he : …	Never	Rarely	Occasionally	Very frequently	Always	Don't know
PLANNING & ORGANIZING						
1. Gets stuck on parts of tasks and can't move forward.			✓			
2. Becomes overwhelmed by too many options or large tasks.				✓		
3. Needs to be told to start a task even when interested in doing it.			✓			
4. Leaves his belongings messy and disorganized.				✓		
5. Has trouble figuring out where to start an activity or task.			✓			
INHIBITORY CONTROL						
1. Fails to stop <u>himself</u> from doing unsafe or inappropriate things (like running into the street, grabbing something from another person).		✓				
2. Has difficulty managing worry or disappointment.		✓				
3. Is easily distracted by noises, activity, sights, <u>other</u> people.				✓		
4. Has difficulty delaying rewards or events.			✓			
5. Gives up easily.			✓			
Subtotal 1	0	2	5	1	2	0

Compared to other children my child's age, s/he : …	Never	Rarely	Occasionally	Very frequently	Always	Don't know
WORKING MEMORY						
1. Only remembers one thing when given tasks.		✓				
2. Forgets what he is supposed to get when sent to fetch something.		✓				
3. Becomes overwhelmed by too much information.			✓			
4. Has difficulty retelling or re-enacting stories or events.		✓				
5. Doesn't remember the names of other children.		✓				
SELF-MONITORING						
1. Does not check for mistakes in his work or activities.				✓		
2. Makes careless errors.					✓	
3. Is unaware of how his behavior affects or impacts other people.				✓		
4. Does not check his progress when doing a task or activity.						✓
5. Does not check back to the goal of a task to refresh his memory.			✓			
COGNITIVE FLEXIBILITY						
1. Tries the same approach to a problem again and again even when it doesn't work.			✓			
2. Is upset by new situations, people or activities.			✓			
3. Resists change in plans, routines, food, clothes, etc.		✓				
4. Locks in on a topic or activity and sticks with it even after others have moved on.		✓				
5. Has difficulty making smooth transitions from activity to activity or place to place.	✓					
Subtotal 2	1	6	4	3	1	1
Total (Subtotal 1 + 2)	1	8	9	3	3	1

These results show that six items are marked 'very frequently' or 'always'. He seems to have most problems in Planning & Organization and Self-monitoring. 'Occasionally' was checked in all executive function categories which supports the need for improved self-regulation.

The survey results clearly indicate that he needs to work on his self-regulation. There's nothing 'wrong' with him but life could be easier with stronger self-regulation.

Jack's mom reads on.

ILLUSTRATION – four year old girl (Emma)

Emma is a four year old girl. Her mom completed the Executive Function Survey. Here are the results:

EXECUTIVE FUNCTION SURVEY

Please put a check (✓) in the column that tells how often you've seen your child behave in the way described by the sentence as <u>compared to other children his/her age.</u>

Child's name: Emma   Today's date: June, 2015

Person completing survey: Sandra   Relation to child: Mom

Compared to other children my child's age, s/he :...	Never	Rarely	Occasionally	Very frequently	Always	Don't know
PLANNING & ORGANIZING						
1.→ Gets stuck on parts of tasks and can't move forward.	✓					
2.→ Becomes overwhelmed by too many options or large tasks.					✓	
3.→ Needs to be told to start a task even when interested in doing it.		✓				
4.→ Leaves his belongings messy and disorganized.					✓	
5.→ Has trouble figuring out where to start an activity or task.		✓				
INHIBITORY CONTROL						
1.→ Fails to stop himself from doing unsafe or inappropriate things (like running into the street, grabbing something from another person).				✓		
2.→ Has difficulty managing worry or disappointment.				✓		
3.→ Is easily distracted by noises, activity, sights, other people.				✓		
4.→ Has difficulty delaying rewards or events.				✓		
5.→ Gives up easily.		✓				
Subtotal 1	1	3	1	3	2	0

Compared to other children my child's age, s/he :...	Never	Rarely	Occasionally	Very frequently	Always	Don't know
WORKING MEMORY						
1.→ Only remembers one thing when given tasks.		✓				
2.→ Forgets what he is supposed to get when sent to fetch something.		✓				
3.→ Becomes overwhelmed by too much information.			✓			
4.→ Has difficulty retelling or re-enacting stories or events.		✓				
5.→ Doesn't remember the names of other children.		✓				
SELF-MONITORING						
1.→ Does not check for mistakes in his work or activities.				✓		
2.→ Makes careless errors.					✓	
3.→ Is unaware of how his behavior affects or impacts other people.				✓		
4.→ Does not check his progress when doing a task or activity.				✓		
5.→ Does not check back to the goal of a task to refresh his memory.		✓				
COGNITIVE FLEXIBILITY						
1.→ Tries the same approach to a problem again and again even when it doesn't work.		✓				
2.→ Is upset by new situations, people or activities.		✓				
3.→ Resists change in plans, routines, food, clothes, etc.				✓		
4.→ Looks in on a topic or activity and sticks with it even after others have moved on.		✓				
5.→ Has difficulty making smooth transitions from activity to activity or place to place.			✓			
Subtotal 2	0	8	3	4	1	0
Total (Subtotal 1 + 2)	1	11	4	6	3	0

These results show that nine items are marked 'very frequently' or 'always'. Emma seems to have most problems in Planning & Organization, Inhibitory Control and Self-monitoring. There are also some 'occasionally' responses in Working Memory and Cognitive Flexibility.

The survey results clearly indicate that she needs to work on self-regulation. There's nothing wrong with her, just like Jack, but she won't struggle so much with life when she has stronger self-regulation.

Emma's mom reads on.

2 Where to start?

Executive functions and self-regulation typically develop and mature over a fairly long period of time. We see the infant sucking his fingers and thumb to regulate and soothe himself and that's just the beginning. Developing and refining self-regulation takes place over at least the first two decades of life. In addition, each of the five executive functions develops at different paces; some maturing earlier, some later.

Notice in the graph below that self-regulation usually shows large improvements during the preschool years. There is some change from that point to the teenage years and then there's a small dip. After that, there's still some continuing refinement but we see a drop-off after

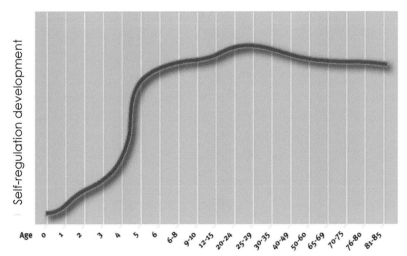

Typical development of self-regulation skills from birth though 85+ years. Notice the accelerated learning through the preschool years and continuation through to about 30 years of age.

about age 30 with a small decline through to the senior years.

Self-regulation develops over at least the first two decades of life. This long period of development means two main things: (1) we have a wide window of time to help our children develop and improve their self-regulation, and (2) we shouldn't expect self-regulation to appear overnight.

Our brains are plastic in the sense that they can change and mold to new experiences. New nerve pathways are developed when we learn and practice new things. Keep in mind that learning to self-regulate takes time and daily practice. This is especially true for children who need to un-learn old ways of doing things and develop new approaches.

Patience and persistence with a dash of good humor are absolutely critical! Start with small steps and skills. Take time to build a solid foundation before moving on to more complex skills. The time you invest will be well worth it.

The spark* Model

The **Self-Regulation Program for Awareness and Resilience in Kids** (spark*)[19] is a step-by-step approach to teaching self-regulation of behavior, thinking processes, and emotions. It was developed over more than 20 years of work with children with special needs but applies to all children.

spark* combines the latest scientific research in the fields of neuroscience, social learning and positive psychology. It's an evidence-based program that is highly effective. Our findings show that children benefit from learning to control their bodies first. This kick-starts improvement in their thinking and social skills[20].

spark* is designed to help children become aware of their ability to control their own bodies, thinking, and emotions. To make sure children develop a firm understanding and solid use of each skill, we always follow these four steps:

1. Increasing self-awareness. This gives him a chance to learn, "I can do it" while practicing the skills and developing solid control.

2. Understanding when and where he needs to use his new skills. He learns, "I can do it here and here." This step helps ensure that your child will use his self-regulation not just at home but at school and other places.

3. Practicing in more challenging places, like noisy, busy settings. He figures out "I can do it even when ..."

4. Advocating for himself. Your child learns to help himself stay regulated even in challenging situations. For example, he might decide to leave a situation if too noisy or busy for him. He learns, "I can help myself by going somewhere quiet."

The three main units of **spark*** are:

1. Body self-regulation

2. Cognitive self-regulation

3. Emotional self-Regulation

spark* goes step by step, building new skills on to those already learned. Body self-regulation is the first. Learning how to calm and focus his whole body gives him a

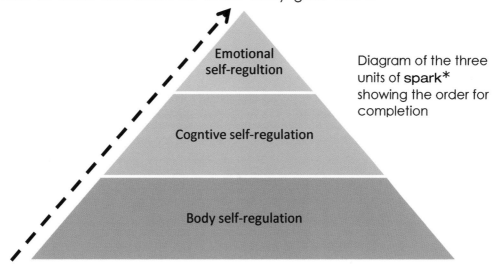

Emotional self-regultion

Cogntive self-regulation

Body self-regulation

Diagram of the three units of **spark*** showing the order for completion better foundation for calming and focusing his brain.

Work on every skill, one at a time to make sure your child is successful before moving to the next. This process is like building a house – you need to make sure you build a solid foundation before adding floors and other structures. Complete the foundation skills in Body self-regulation and then move on to Cognitive self-regulation. Once the cognitive self-regulation are solid, the final structure (Emotional self-regulation) can be added to the solid base.

Body self-regulation

Body self-regulation involves increasing your child's awareness that he has control over his movements, he can resist impulses, and learn when and where different actions are appropriate. In learning to self-regulate his actions, your child discovers that he can vary how, when, and where he uses his body and can do it in flexible ways that work in different settings.

Areas of focus

The main areas of focus on body self-regulation are hands, feet and whole body movements, breathing and voice volume.

The hands, feet and whole body are the first areas. Children often enjoy moving in different ways, especially to music, and we can help them learn to vary them, moving fast, slow, or like a dinosaur or a butterfly. We also practice self-regulation in stop-and-go games, like *What Time is it Mr. Wolf/Fox?* or freeze tag.

Breathing is introduced next. We use breathing as a way for your child to center and calm himself (you'll learn more about it on pages 51-58). We'll use slow Turtle Breathing in all activities as well as in day-to-day life. It's used before starting an activity and when your child becomes over-excited or upset.

Our last focus is voice. Your child will learn that he can change the loudness of his voice in different places (like at a library or soccer game) and at different times (like when someone is sleeping or talking or when calling someone who's far away).

Activity variations

For each area of focus, actions are practiced using different variations. The four main variations include:

1. Speed or rate, such as clapping quickly or breathing slowly.

2. Intensity or force, such as speaking quietly or stomping your feet hard.

3. Manner of movement, such as hopping like a bunny or slithering like a snake.

In the beginning, you'll have him imitate you or other family members. This way, he learns the expectations for each activity, the vocabulary for body parts, and the songs and rhymes. After that, encourage him to 'be teacher' so he takes the lead and teaches others.

Cognitive Self-Regulation

Cognitive self-regulation involves teaching your child how and when to use his thinking resources. You'll help your child learn to gather important information, ignore distractions, check his understanding of information and express his ideas more clearly.

Areas of focus

There are three main areas of focus for Cognitive self-regulation. These involve taking in information, making sense of it and then deciding how to respond. Skills were selected based on their importance to learning, their value to future cognitive development, and their feasibility with young children.

The three areas and skills include:

1. Take in all of the important information

    a. Focus your attention

    b. Figure out what's expected in a situation or activity

2. Put the pieces of information together and check to make sure you understand

3. Explain your thoughts and ideas in clear ways

Our goals are to help your child learn to look carefully at an activity or situation and focus on the important parts. Then we want him to make a picture in his brain and ask himself, "Hmm, what am I supposed to do with this?" He also needs to make sure he understands any directions he hears (for example, "Do I know what to do?", "Does that make sense?"). Then we want him to know how to talk about his ideas so other people will understand him.

Emotional Self-Regulation

Emotional self-regulation involves helping your child find important social clues (facial expressions), figure out what they mean, and then respond in appropriate ways. We want your child to learn to manage his emotions with more flexibility as well as understand other people's behavior. For example, if your child becomes angry at another person, he can regulate his emotions and walk away or tell an adult rather than hitting, yelling or swearing.

The ability to identify emotions and what cause them is more important than most of us realize. Children who can identify emotions and connect them to are more advanced socially[21]. Those who are better at controlling

18

their emotions and behavior when excited or upset are considered more socially competent[22]. Children with more developed emotional self-regulation can cope with emotional ups and downs, maintain their own emotional equilibrium, and recover more easily from setbacks and disappointments[23]. These are the children that others prefer to be with[24].

The Emotional Self-Regulation unit focuses on skills and strategies that form a basis for developing social skills. Among those skills are recognizing and identifying emotions and regulating behavior and reactions to emotional ups and downs.

We don't deny, dismiss or stifle the child's emotions. Instead, he learns to more accurately detect, understand and express emotions with a sense of control and optimism.

Areas of focus

In the Emotional Self-Regulation unit, your child learns to make good social and emotional decisions. Our goals are to help him:

1. Develop self-awareness in recognizing his own emotions

2. Recognize emotions in other people

3. Understand what different emotions mean and what might cause them

4. Manage his emotions.

How we teach the skills

Always start by helping your child understand he has control of how and when he moves his body, thinks and reacts to people around him. We help him learn self-awareness and to become more independent, using the Language of **spark*** (see pages 28 to 31 for an explanation).

When teaching body self-regulation, your child learns he has control of his body. He can decide where his body and parts of his body are as well as the speed, forcefulness and manner of movements. This self-awareness may seem obvious to adults but many children don't realize it. Once he's discovered self-regulation of his body, he can progress to be-coming aware of his thinking and how he can gain conscious con-trol of it. He's then ready to take on emotions. He be-comes more aware of clues provided by others and within himself and how to read and respond to them.

To help bridge the gap between knowing what to do and doing it in everyday life, you'll help your child figure out where and when different actions, thoughts and emotions are appropriate and possible.

The next step is to go into those different places and let your child test his new self-regulation skills. He can build up his resilience that way so he uses the new skills and strategies, even in difficult situations. You'll need to support and prompt him in the beginning stages. After more practice, he'll figure it out for himself but ask for help when he needs it.

ILLUSTRATION – seven year old boy (Jack) - continued

Jack's mom says that he's a pretty good little athlete and has good gross motor skills. He can start and stop and move quickly or slowly in sports so why bother doing the Body self-regulation activities. They seem sort of silly. Also, his main issues are about planning, organization and self-monitoring. His teacher said that he has some problems focusing on his work at school but she can work on that. Why bother starting with Body self-regulation? He needs work on teaching him to pay attention.

Body self-regulation is important because Jack needs to have a solid base of calm control of his body before he can really focus his attention. If he learns how to get a better sense of his body, where it is and how calm it is, he's ready to work on focusing his thinking.

An interesting study was done in the 1960s by Mischel and colleagues. They did an experiment with preschoolers called the marshmallow test. They told the children they could have one mini-marshmallow immediately but, if they waited, they could have two. The followed the children over the next four decades and found some remarkable differences between the children who could self-regulate and those who took the marshmallow right away. There were significant psychological, behavioral, health and economic outcomes for the children with greater self-regulation. The showed higher academic, greater sense of self-worth and better social and emotional coping.

This research, along with our own, shows that when children develop conscious control of their bodies, they're more able to use their cognitive abilities. We found that children who worked on their body self-regulation for just a few weeks, showed improvement in their cognitive and social skills. This told us kids need to have their body under control and calm in order to focus their attention, work systematically, think things through, etc. They don't just dive in and hope for the best.

Jack's mom reads on.

If you're interested in learning more about Mischel's work, read this article:

Mischel, W., Ayduk, O., Berman, M., Casey, B., Gotlib, I., Jonides, J., Shoda, Y. (2011). "Willpower" over the life span: decomposing self-regulation. *Social Cognitive and Affective Neuroscience*, 6(2), 252–6.

ILLUSTRATION – four year old girl (Emma) - continued

Emma's mom finds that she controls here body pretty well when she dances and plays outside. She takes ballet lessons and can move quickly and slowly. Mom's wondering why she can't just skip ahead to yoga or to Cognitive Self-regulation.

Body Self-regulation is important because Emma needs to have a solid base of conscious control of her body. She needs to develop awareness that she is in control of her body, what it does and where. Emma may be able to run and dance but does she know the extent of the command she has over her body? She also needs to develop a sense of calm so she can quieten her body and her mind. That will make it easier for her to develop cognitive and emotional self-regulation.

The work done by Mischel and his colleagues along with our own research (described on the previous page) provide compelling information on the need to work on body self-regulation.

Emma's mom reads on.

3 Getting ready

How we do things is often as important as what we do. In this chapter, we'll look at some important things to keep in mind when you work on self-regulation with your child.

Make sure your child CAN learn

Before starting any work on self-regulation, make sure your child CAN learn, that is, he is **C**alm, **A**lert and **N**ourished.

Calm means that stress is at a minimum. If your child is feeling stressed, his ability to think can shut down and he'll be less able to explore and learn. Start your work on self-regulation when your child is at his calmest. Once you've established some self-regulation, you can move your practice into other, more stimulating situations.

> *My child has difficulty being or staying calm most of the time so how can I practice with him?*
>
> Think about when he tends to be relaxed. It may be when he's in the bathtub, in the car, in a small space like under a table or on a swing. Complete the form on the next page about where your child feels most calm and relaxed. That's where you'll start your work on self-regulation. Once he gains some skills, move to other settings.

Alertness comes from being well-rested. Most children in the two- to eight-year-old range need 10 to 12 hours of sleep each night. This doesn't always happen. When your child is tired or isn't feeling well, it's not a good time to work on self-regulation.

Times and places when my child tends to be calm. Check (✓) all that apply and add your own.	
In the car	
Walking in the park	
In bed	
In a small space	
On a swing	
Other(s)	

Self-regulation takes energy. Your child's energy and focus will be depleted after practicing so take breaks. Give him time when he can just be himself and not worry about self-regulation. That means giving him time when he can just 'let loose'.

Nourishment about every two to two-and-one-half hours is important to fuel learning. Children need to eat every couple of hours to keep their energy up. Your child needs vegetables, fruit and protein to grow and to help them concentrate. If he's hungry, behavior problems are more likely. Don't work on self-regulation if he's hungry. It'll be too challenging for him and for you.

Although diet changes in children take careful planning, patience, and time, it's essential to appreciate the impact of nutrition on learning. Address it when and where possible.

There are a few tools on the market that can help improve your child's diet and nutrition. One that is well-organized and focuses on children learning to self-regulate is called the *Eating Game* (Game stands for Get-Awesome-Meals-Everyday).

It's been used successfully by many families and helps achieve a more balanced diet. Find out more about it at http://theeatinggame.ca/.

If your child is tired, not feeling well, or hungry, his ability to self-regulate will be lessened. Decide when to practice based on whether he CAN.

Keep learning fun

Children learn better when there's fun involved. We adults also enjoy doing things with our children when there's a good element of fun.

Use music and favorite rhymes to add energy to practicing. Keep success high with just enough challenge to keep your child interested. When starting out, strive for error-free learning so your child doesn't make mistakes and experiences lots of success. Then ask for more. It's important to make sure your child is successful but we also need him to understand that learning takes time, effort, and persistence.

If your child doesn't seem interested in doing an activity, there may be many different reasons. Don't just think he's being lazy, isn't motivated, is stubborn and lacks ability. First, figure out what your child likes and what he doesn't care for. Complete the *Likes and Dislikes Survey* on the next page. Check with your child to make sure you're up-to-date. Use this list to decide activities he'll enjoy most. Start there.

	Likes & Dislikes Survey	
Date:		
Child's name:		
To make sure activities are interesting and fun, please indicate videos, movies, games, etc. that he really likes and those s/he dislikes (so they can be avoided).		
	Really Likes	**Really Dislikes**
Videos or movies		
Games		
TV shows		
Computer programs		
Books		
Toys		
Characters from videos, TV, games,		
Music, musician/artist		
Other(s)		

Using rewards isn't a first choice in motivating children. They're used very sparingly because they can actually decrease your child's intrinsic motivation and the sense of independence[25]. Intrinsic motivation is the drive to do things for the challenge or out of curiosity (for example, some people do crossword puzzles just for the mental exercise and not for an external reward). As a parent, you want your child to be motivated by challenge, curiosity or a sense of accomplishment. It takes positive experiences and time for children to develop intrinsic motivation. Rewards used sparingly in the beginning can bring on more positive experiences that can feed your child's intrinsic motivation.

My child doesn't like the activity I chose

If you start an activity and your child doesn't seem interested:

- Do another activity

- Let your child choose from two or three different options

- Practice another time or in another place

- Use small rewards or 'pay-offs' for doing the activity

Always assume that a problem stems from how you presented something to your child and not a problem with your child. More often than not, you'll be right. Don't feel like you need to rescue your child or do the activity for him. It's okay to let your child struggle a little with a task before helping him or changing the activity.

Make sure your child is thinking

When you work on self-regulation, your child has to be calm, alert and nourished. He also needs to be engaged and thinking. We don't want him simply waiting for us to make decisions for him. We want him participating, having fun, and using his 'good brain' – always tell your child he has a good brain, this lets him know you have faith in his abilities.

The main way we do this is with the **Language of spark***. We've chosen specific words and phrases designed to engage children in activities and thinking. The Language of spark* focuses on both cognitive and social-emotional goals.

Three cognitive goals

These goals emphasize engaging and activating your child's thinking. They include helping him:

1. **Understand the meaning and purpose** of each activity – children are more likely to be interested in activities if they see some purpose. When teaching self-regulation, explain why you're doing activities and why you're using different strategies. In the body, cognitive and emotional self-regulation units, you'll find words and phrases you can use to describe the meaning and purpose of activities.

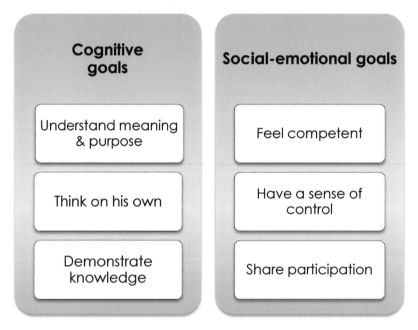

Cognitive goals
- Understand meaning & purpose
- Think on his own
- Demonstrate knowledge

Social-emotional goals
- Feel competent
- Have a sense of control
- Share participation

2. **Think on his own** – we promote independence and help your child become more self-sufficient. Give your child time to think (don't hurry him!). Don't feel mean if you let him struggle a bit. Be patient and calm and let him think and try things out. Mistakes are an excellent opportunity for learning.

   Use questions to prompt your child (for example, "What can you do to help yourself?"). Questions are effective for getting him to think about what he's doing. We want him to learn to ask himself these questions; for example, "What am I supposed to do here?" or "How did I do?"

Offer hints when your child seems stuck. Tell him, "Using both hands together seems to work better for you" or "It might be easier if you did this part first".

Encourage your child to keep working. Saying, "You can do it." or "You're really close." can be powerful.

There are more suggestions to help you in the chapters ahead.

3. **Demonstrate his knowledge** - When you give your child freedom and confidence to do things on his own, you'll learn more about what he really knows and can do. Children often surprise us when we give them a chance.

   In each unit that follows, you'll find suggestions for prompting your child to show and explain what he's learned.

Three social-emotional goals

These goals focus on developing more independence and confidence in your child. They include helping him:

1. **Feel competent -** A child's sense of competence comes from experiencing success. That's why we use things he likes and keep your sessions fun. We also make sure your child is successful. The positive language we use encourages him to keep working. Even if he does something you weren't expecting or something that wasn't correct, respond positively. If he says or does something you didn't expect, comment, "Hmm, that's really interesting. Can you help me understand?" If his response isn't accurate, say, "Gee, I'm not sure. Can we do that again?" or "That doesn't look like what I got. Let's check it out." Avoid negative words, like "no", "not" and "don't". They stop thinking and can undermine your child's confidence and cooperation. Always use positive language; rather than saying, "Don't do that", say "How about if we do it this way?"

2. **Have a sense of control** - Every child wants a sense of control. He wants to move from being regulated

by you to becoming self-regulated. This doesn't mean that your child is free to do whatever he wants. He has to learn personal responsibility along with his sense of control.

We want your child to become the commander of his own body, thinking, and emotions. To help him do that, we talk about how he controlled his feet, hands, voice, body, brain, etc. or forgot to do it. The focus on body parts rather than him alone helps him understand that he has control of them. It also preserves his feelings of competence by separating his central self from his body parts. It sets a boundary

between your child and his behavior. It gives him the message that he continues to be a strong and positive force in the world but his hands, feet, voice, whole body and/or his brain sometimes forget to do things.

3.   **Share participation** – When working with your child, use the word "we" frequently. It signals shared participation between you and your child (for example, "We need to ..."). It also emphasizes that learning self-regulation is a joint effort for the two of you. Your child's not alone in needing to work on self-regulation. It's reassuring for your child to hear you say that other people need to work on their self-regulation as well.

Another way to share participation is to let your child choose what to do, how and/or when. This gives him a feeling of participating rather than being told what to do. The choices can be simple: you decide which activities but your child decides the order for doing them.

Avoid ordering your child to "Stop doing that!" or "Do this." It makes your relationship with your child one-sided – he listens and you tell him what to do. Provide suggestions, starting with, "Let's ..." or "How about we ...?", rather than telling him what to do. He'll learn from this model too and find ways to soften his own requests.

> *My child doesn't want to do an activity I know he likes*
>
> Sometimes children need warm-up time before an activity. Try starting the activity on your own. Even if your child doesn't appear interested, he'll see you're having fun. One way to get him involved is to make an error on purpose or forget part of the activity. Chances are, he'll jump in to help you.

Use the "180 degree rule": turn a negative into a positive. This means turning your feelings and thoughts to the opposite direction. You turn "Stop that" into "You can do this". For example, you want your child to stop running around. Instead of saying, "Stop running!", you calm yourself and say, "We walk in the house". Instead of saying, "Don't grab your sister's toy.", say "We use gentle hands with our toys." Often children know what not to do but don't know what they should do instead. Using the "180 degree rule" helps your child learn positive alternatives while you stay calm and positive and focus on what you want rather than what you don't want.

Be a model

You can be an example for your child by using the strategies he's learning. This can be done positively or negatively.

As a positive model, you show what to do and/or talk to yourself about things you need to remember. For example, think out loud: "I want to make a sandwich so I'll need some bread and some ..." This shows how you plan and organize things. You can also talk about how you regulate your body. For example, "I need to tell my fingers to be very careful with that knife because I could cut myself. Be careful hands!"

With a negative model, you show your child how sometimes you forget to use self-regulation. Maybe you walk too fast up the stairs and stumble. You can comment, "Go slower feet. That way we won't get hurt." It's really important for your child to understand that everyone, even adults, have a hard time controlling their bodies sometimes. Hearing this from you will help him feel like he's not the only person in the world who needs to work on self-regulation.

> ### My child can't do an activity
>
> If your child is unsuccessful with an activity, do it two or three more times, each time changing the amount and type of support you give him. If your child continues to have difficulty, move on to something else. Doing another activity is NOT giving in. It's the smart thing to do. You can always introduce the first activity again on another day.
>
> Ask your child what he'd like to do or how he'd like to do that activity. Follow his lead. This models being flexible and following someone's lead. You can suggest doing the activity your way next time.

Children sense when adults are stressed or anxious. We talked about how your child should be calm when working on self-regulation. The same is true for you. The calmer you are when practicing self-regulation with your child, the more likely it'll be positive and successful. Before practicing self-regulation with your child, take a few minutes to calm yourself. It's important for both you and your child.

Remember that learning is a process

All learning takes time and practice. Many children need time to think about new things they're learning and to try them on their own.

First, we need to make sure your child learns skills solidly and understands why they're important. Practice is the road to becoming an expert and that takes time. Your child will need your help celebrating his improving performance. Start helping your child use his skills at home and in the community. It's important to remember that, even though he might do something when practicing with you, he may not use it in everyday life.

Teaching and practice that are fun and positive are never wasted. It takes time, though, to make that learning solid and useable in everyday life. We all make mistakes when we're learning. Be positive and know that, in the long run, your child will improve.

Make sure you and your child enjoy the activities you do and you both finish up happy and satisfied. Follow this simple rule: the number of minutes you do an activity should be no more than two times your child's age. Have a look at the table below.

If your child is	Do activities for <u>no more than:</u>
2 to 3 years of age	4 to 6 minutes
3 to 4 years of age	6 to 8 minutes
4 to 5 years of age	8 to 10 minutes
5 to 6 years of age	10 to 12 minutes
6 to 8 years of age	12 to 14 minutes

Note to the reader:

As you read this chapter, you may have noticed a number of things. Things like, "Wow, I really have to stop and remember not to just do things for my child if he's slow or not doing something the way I like." You're right.

You need to use your own self-regulation. Remember to exercise your own executive functions in order to help your child. For example,

- Planning and organization –

    o Make sure you have the time to do the activity you planned.

    o Make sure you and your child aren't tired or hungry when you practice.

    o Include things he likes and enjoys.

- Inhibitory control –

    o Make sure you're calm.

    o Don't dive into an activity. Be sure to explain its meaning and purpose.

    o Let him try things on his own, even if he makes mistakes or something isn't exactly how you like it.

- Working memory –

    o Keep all the features and examples of the Language of spark* in mind while you work with your child. The cue cards on the Resources site will help you.

- Self-monitoring –

    o Make sure you're using the Language of spark*. We can't emphasize enough how important the Language of spark* is to your child's learning self-regulation.

    o Think out loud to model your own self-regulation for your child.

- Cognitive flexibility –

    o Be able to flow with things even though they may not turn out the way you expected or your child didn't say or do what you intended.

    o Use the 180 degree rule, turning negative feelings and thoughts around to positive ones.

ILLUSTRATION – seven year old boy (Jack) - continued

Jack's mom completed the survey of likes and dislikes. Here it is:

Likes & Dislikes		
Date: June, 2015		
Child's name: Jack		
To make sure activities are interesting and fun, please indicate videos, movies, games, etc. that he really likes and those s/he dislikes (so they can be avoided).		
	Really Likes	**Really Dislikes**
Videos or movies	YouTube, the sillier the better	Babyish or 'girl' movies
Games	Active sports (hockey, lacrosse)	
TV shows	Active 'rude' cartoons like "The Day my Butt went Psycho", "Johnny Test"	
Computer programs	Minecraft	
Books		
Toys	Action figures	'girl' toys
Characters from videos, TV, games, books	Johnny Test	Characters from 'girl' movies, etc,
Music, musician/artist	Just about anything	
Other(s)	Being first Being best, fastest at something	Being put on the spot Making mistakes in front of other people

It looks like Jack likes highly stimulating activities, movies, etc. especially ones that are 'rude' and silly – not unusual for boys. He's also a pretty sensitive guy who doesn't like to be made an example of. It seems like modeling skills, strategies and mistakes could be a good way to help him in addition to direct instruction.

ILLUSTRATION – four year old girl (Emma) – continued

Emma's mom completed the survey of likes and dislikes. Here it is:

Likes & Dislikes		
Date: June, 2015		
Child's name: Emma		
To make sure activities are interesting and fun, please indicate videos, movies, games, etc. that he really likes and those s/he dislikes (so they can be avoided).		
	Really Likes	**Really Dislikes**
Videos or movies	Animal movies	Barbie, princess movies
Games	Active outdoor activities, swimming,	
TV shows	Word Girl, Angelina Ballerina	
Computer programs		
Books	Animal stories	
Toys	horses	dolls
Characters from videos, TV, games, books	Just about any animal	
Music, musician/artist	Classical music	
Other(s)	Doing things quickly	Being 'pushed' into new situations or meeting new people – needs time to warm up

It looks like Emma likes active games. She loves animals, especially horses. She doesn't seem to be into 'traditional' girl toys and tends to prefer books about strong characters (in addition to animals, of course!). She is considered 'shy' by people who just meet her but she's outgoing with people she knows, especially other children.

4 Body self-regulation

The Body self-regulation unit comes first because it forms a foundation for Cognitive and Emotional self-regulation.

In the Body self-regulation unit, our goals are to help your child:

1. learn that he can control when, where and how he moves his body,

2. practice self-regulating his body even in challenging situations,

3. help himself if he feels he's becoming un-regulated or stressed, and

4. begin using slow breathing to calm and center himself.

In the information that follows, you'll learn more about each goal, where and when you might practice the skills with your child, activities you can do with him to improve his self-regulation, and resources you can use. Remember, you can move on to another area but still practice things you've done before.

Use everyday situations, like while you're driving the car (please be careful to give proper attention to your driving, however) or going for a walk. It's more fun to include other children and adults whenever you can – the more the merrier! We keep special materials to a minimum – any extras you might need will be on the Self-regulation Everyday website (http://www.self-reg-everyday.com). Keep expenses to a minimum - suggested storybooks can be borrowed from your local library.

Order of skills

1. Start by helping your child learn to control his **body and body parts** at different speeds, intensities (lightly or with a lot of force) and in different ways (for example, like a butterfly or an angry bear).

2. Our next area is learning to use slow steady **breathing** to calm and center himself. You and your child will use Turtle Breathing. This is slow, steady breathing in and out of your nose or mouth. Some children have a difficult time figuring out how to breathe just through their noses so we'll accept breathing through his mouth in the beginning.

3. Next, we focus on self-regulation of **voice** volume. You and your child can have fun singing songs and rhymes loudly, softly and somewhere in between.

Self-Regulation of hands, feet and whole body

Stage 1 – I can do it!

The goal of these activities is to help your child learn that he can control his hands, feet and whole body and move them at different speeds, intensities, and manners all by himself. The main executive functions practiced at this stage are:

- inhibitory control - your child has to change speed, intensity and manner of movement and stop himself from moving in other ways

- self-monitoring - asking him what he thinks about his actions (for example, "How did your hands do that time?").

For Stage 1, introduce and practice self-regulation doing things your child enjoys. Go back to page 26 to review your child's likes and dislikes. Use songs, rhythm and music whenever possible. Music often engages children and prompts them to participate.

ACTIVITIES

Choose a safe place for practicing. If your child is running around, make sure he won't fall or run into difficulty. Some children are very conscious of being watched so choose a private space for just the two of you to practice. You can practice in the car when driving, in the bathtub, while waiting in lines or just about anywhere.

Different speeds: Remind your child that you can move quickly or slowly. Ask your child how he wants to move. Let him decide and do the action, rhyme or song at his pace. Partway through, change the speed, and add in "stop" and "go". Have fun and keep it playful.

Different intensities: Tell your child that sometimes you can do actions to songs and/or movements really hard and sometimes really softly. Ask your child to choose how he wants to do the activity: hard or soft. Let him decide and do it his way. Part way through, change the intensity. Take turns with your child deciding on the intensity and mixing in some changes of speed.

Different manners: Tell your child that sometimes you can move like creatures. You can do actions like a bunny, a butterfly or a bear. Ask your child how he wants move. Show pictures of creatures in the beginning, particularly with younger children. An assortment of pictures is in the resources on the Self-regulation Everyday website (www.self-reg-everyday.com) – you can also use stuffed animals, puppets and action figures. Let him decide and do actions like that creature. Part way, change the creature. Take turns with your child deciding on the

> Language of spark*
> ....
> Introduce the activity with "Let's .." or "How about we ...?" These emphasize shared participation.
>
> Give feelings of competence by telling your child, "You really know how to control your ......"
>
> Increase your child's sense of control by letting him decide the speed, intensity or manner of action.

creature and mix in some changes of speed and intensity also.

Play imitation games, like *Follow the Leader,* and songs using different speeds, intensities and manners. These will improve your child's body self-regulation and encourage imitation.

Many suggested materials and resources are on the Resources page of the Self-regulation Everyday website. There are materials and resources suitable for all children from two through eight years of age.

Example ▶ (in the car – please be very careful about doing activities while driving and only do them if they don't take your mind off the road) "Let's sing *If You're Happy and You Know It* (check the Resources files on the website if your memory needs refreshing). Are you ready?" Sing one round with your child, then suggest, "How about we do that again but clap really loudly?" Sing the round again. "Okay, let's do the next part really fast. Are you ready?" Sing the next round. "Wow, you really controlled your hands and told them what to do. Well done! (OR "It looks like you have to tell your hands what to do. Let's tell them, hands, you need to clap fast") How do you want to do the actions for the next one, stomping your feet quietly, loudly, slowly or fast?" Sing the next round doing the actions the way your child chose. "Nice job! You really told your feet what to do. (OR "Keep trying. Those silly feet need to listen better. You tell them.") Okay, let's do one more round. How should we do the actions this time?" After the next round, ask "How did your feet and hands do this time?" If his judgement of his performance was accurate, praise him. If it wasn't very well done, say, "Hmm, it didn't look like the best they can do. Let's do it again and really watch how your feet/hands work."

Example ▶ (walking to the park) "Let's walk like rabbits. How about we do it five times? Let's do it." Hop five times, counting each hop with your child. "How should we walk this time, like a dinosaur, a fairy, a kangaroo, a bear? How many steps should we take?" Move in the way your child suggests. "Let's walk really fast until I say to stop." Walk quickly, eventually saying "Stop". "Ha-ha, I caught you! Tell your feet to stop as soon as you hear "Stop".

ILLUSTRATION – seven year old boy (Jack) - continued

Jack's mom is worried that he's going to think these activities are 'stupid' and 'babyish'. What to do? There are lots of 'gross' songs and rhymes for older children in the resources – remember "Great green gobs of greasy grimy gopher guts"? Jack'd like that kind of song. Put some actions to it and he'd practice. Just be sure to talk to him about his ability to control his body. He needs to be consciously aware of it.

He also likes YouTube and some contemporary music. Try different actions ... and, of course, dancing ... to them. Actions to songs like Gangnam Style would be perfect. The idea is to control where and how your body moves.

Jack's mom could also find CDs he likes and slow the music down, speed it up, or stop it so he has to listen and control his body.

He probably would be willing to help a younger child learn these skills. He seems to like being the 'big guy' and 'teacher' so helping someone else could probably get him engaged. This would be a good way to get him to talk about times and places when he needs to control his body and when he can let loose.

He'll probably pick this up pretty quickly. Move on to Stages 3 and 4 whenever you can. That's where you can coach him to help himself and praise him for his attempts.

Along the way, Mom should make his teacher aware of their work on self-regulation. She should update her along the way so the teacher can keep an eye open for changes. The teacher can also remind Jack of strategies if appropriate and she might even have the rest of the children join in.

ILLUSTRATION – four year old girl (Emma) – continued

Emma loves dancing to classical music so planning activities isn't a problem. She may balk at moving in different ways and at different speeds but, if you let her tell others what to do, she'll probably be okay.

Emma should enjoy most of the songs and games included in the Resources site as well.

Mom should keep Emma's preschool teacher updated on things they're doing in self-regulation. The teacher can watch out for changes and try out some of the strategies in the classroom.

Now you can tell me how to walk and when to stop. Are you ready? How do you want to walk, fast, slow, tiptoeing, stomping?" Once he decides how to walk, start off and wait for him to say "Stop". If he forgets, pretend you're exhausted and remind him to say "Stop". Praise him for controlling his feet and body. As you practice more, ask your child, "How did your body do that time?" If he's accurate in his evaluation, say, "I agree, I think you did a wonderful job of telling your body what to do." If his judgement isn't accurate, say, "Well, I'm not sure. I think your body could probably do a little better. Let's give it another go and be sure to watch your body really carefully."

Stage 2 – I can do it here and here

Move on to this stage when your child shows that he can easily move his hands, feet and body at different speeds, with different intensities, and in different manners. Continue practicing like you did in Stage 1 whenever you can – it's fun and good for everyone.

The goal of this stage is to help your child understand where and when he can use different speeds, intensities and manners of movement. The main executive functions focused on at this stage are:

- inhibitory control - your child has to change speed, intensity and manner of movement and stop himself from moving in other ways

- planning and organization - thinking ahead to different locations and what changes in movement might be needed

- working memory - comparing each situation to rules about how to move

- cognitive flexibility - changing how he moves his body dependent on the situation

Language of spark*

Understanding meaning and purpose is encouraged by asking, "Why do you think that's a good/not so good idea?"

Prompt him to think on his own by asking questions like, "What should you tell your (body part)?" and "How can we help ourselves remember?"

Help your child feel competent with statements like, "Good thinking!", "How did you know what to do?", "You're so clever."

ACTIVITIES

Talk to your child about when he can run, when he should walk, when he should move slowly, when he should tiptoe, and when he can move like a bunny. Use situations at home and in the community to practice (for example, at the grocery store, at the shopping mall, at religious services).

Example → "I'm thinking about what we need to do with our bodies in different places. How about if (person) is having a nap? What should we tell our bodies to do?" Act out the situation as needed. Let your child take a turn being the sleeping person. Stomp your feet as you walk by. Then

ask him, "Hmm, do you think that would be a good idea? What should I tell my feet to do?" If he chooses telling his feet to walk quietly, praise him. If he's not sure, act out an exaggerated scene with your child pretending to sleep and you stomping your feet. Ask, "Is it easy to sleep when I'm making so much noise? It's really difficult, isn't it? We need to tell our feet to walk quietly. How can you help yourself remember to use quiet feet when someone's sleeping?" Accept any suggestion your child makes. You can also suggest things that you might use to remind yourself. Explore other places, where he can run and stomp (like the playground) or where he needs to control his body (for example, a place of worship, doctor's office).

Introduce storybooks with characters moving in different ways that are appropriate (like the gingerbread man who's running away) and inappropriate. Discuss these characters and their choices about moving their bodies in different ways. Talk about why and where it's appropriate. You'll find suggestions for different storybooks in the resources on the Self-regulation Everyday website (www.self-reg-everyday.com) that are suitable for children from two through eight years of age.

You could have fun putting together a little storybook or video that shows him moving his body in ways appropriate to different settings. Draw pictures or make a video of him walking quietly in a library, running in a gym or playground, or using soft hands when petting the family pet. Storybooks and videos are excellent ways to let your child review things he's learned.

When you're at home or out in the community with your child, comment about how he's controlling his body or letting loose. If he forgets to regulate his body, say, "It looks like your hands/feet/body forgot what to do. What do you need to tell your hands/feet/body?" Point out when you forget to control your body and model how you remind yourself.

Stage 3 – I can do it even when ...

Move on to this stage after your child shows he understands that he can move his body in different ways in different places - where he can let loose and where he needs more control. Practice like you did in Stage 1 whenever you can – it's fun and good for everyone.

The goal of this stage is to help your child cope in situations that might challenge his self-regulation. The main executive functions focused on at this stage are:

- inhibitory control – he can control his body even with temptations, distractions and other influences

---

Language of spark*

Prompt your child to think on his own with comments like, "You really told your hands what to do. What did you tell them?" Model statements like, "Hands, you need to help Mom with the groceries right now."

Help your child feel competent with statements like, "Good thinking!", "You really know how to tell your hands, body, feet what to do."

ILLUSTRATION – seven year old boy (Jack) - continued

Jack has a tendency to grab things from other people and wander off in stores. His mom focuses on those issues with him.

She also asks him for suggestions. He can think of lots of ideas for other people. His mom decides to help him figure out how to help them use their self-regulation in different places. This is a great opportunity to talk about the need for different behaviors in different places. Remember, Jack doesn't like being singled out so focusing on other people will be a lot easier for him. It'll still give Jack a chance to talk about changes in self-regulation for different settings.

ILLUSTRATION – four year old girl (Emma) – continued

Emma is often a force to be reckoned with. She's usually slow to warm up to new situations and people and fairly bold around people she knows. This is a chance to work on both.

In new situations, she often hides behind her parent. She could work on standing beside them. That can be one way she regulates her body.

In familiar settings, she can get a little pushy with other children. Discussions and rehearsals can center around situations like that and how she can control her hands, feet and body. She would respond well to storybooks that present characters that have difficulty with body self-regulation, acting out the parts.

- working memory – he remembers what he's supposed to do in different settings

- self-monitoring - checking to make sure he's controlling his body or letting loose, depending on the situation

- cognitive flexibility - changing his self-regulation depending on the situation

ACTIVITIES

Now that your child has practiced the different skills and understands why and where they're important, it's time to take them on the road. Choose places that are safe even if your child forgets to control his hands, feet, or body. These should increasingly be places where he had difficulty regulating himself in the past.

You can do some preventive work with your child by talking to him about the things he has to remind his hands, feet or body to do. For example, "We're going to the grocery store and you remember the last time that your hands kept trying to put some candy in our cart. I said that we didn't need any candy. What could you tell your hands this time?" You can help your child control his body by engaging him in something that will keep him busy. Have him push the grocery cart, hold the grocery list and check to make sure you buy everything on it, holding groceries or helping to put them on the conveyor at the check-out.

Example (in the grocery store where your child usually picks up a candy bar at the checkout) Catch him before he touches the candy bars and say, "Wow, look how you told your hands to control themselves and how you just looked at the candy bars. That's fantastic! Good for you! Well done!" (I don't believe you can lay on too much praise for work well done). "What did you tell your hands?"

Example (in the mall where he usually runs ahead of you) If he starts to run ahead, stop him and ask, "What do you need to tell your body?" If he's unsure, remind him how you talked about staying together at the mall so you can see him (remember, you have to give it meaning and purpose). Ask him again, "What do you need to tell your body?" If he's still not sure, ask what would happen if he runs ahead (you can't see where he is and that makes you worry). Then ask him one more time, "What do you need to tell your body?" If he doesn't have an answer, tell him, "Body, you need to slow down and stay with Mom." You could also help keep him with you by engaging him in activities like pushing a cart or carrying shopping bags. These tasks will help slow him down a little and give you a chance to notice and praise his self-regulation. Stay especially alert with younger children and be ready to step in front of him or take hold of his shirt if needed to stop him.

Stage 4 – I can help myself by ...

Move on to this stage when your child shows he can control his body most of the time in important places. He doesn't have to have perfect control – it's a work in progress.

The goal of this stage is to help your child support his own self-regulation in different settings by advocating for himself. The main executive functions focused on at this stage are:

- inhibitory control – he controls his body even when there are distractions and temptations

- planning and organization - thinking ahead about how he can help himself and keep himself under control

- working memory - comparing the present situation to rules about self-regulation and how he might help himself

- self-monitoring - checking to see how he's doing with his self-regulation

- cognitive flexibility - changing his self-regulation for different situations

Language of spark*
....
Prompt your child to think on his own with comments like, "What can you do to help yourself?"

Give your child many opportunities to demonstrate his new skills. Stand back and let it happen.

ACTIVITIES

Now that your child has practiced self-regulation in different places with your support, it's time for him to take over more control. Go places you often go (grocery store, place of worship, preschool or school, shopping mall). Be ready to prompt him to think of ways to help himself if he's having a difficult time controlling his hands, feet or body. No matter what he suggests (it may not be what you had in mind), if it'll help, let him do it. He might say something that sounds ridiculous (like, "I can hold my ear and that'll help my body stay still"), let him give it a go. It might just help. Ideas your child comes up with are usually more powerful for him than ones you suggest.

Example → (at a movie theatre and he's squirming in his seat) Put your hand on his shoulder and quietly say, "It looks like your body's having a hard time staying still. (NOTICE: we avoided using a negative like "Your body is squirming all over the place" and we avoided directly referring to him as in "You're squirming all over the place"). What could you do to help yourself?" If he comes up with an idea, praise him. If he has no idea, suggest something like, "You know when I have a hard time keeping my body still, I talk to it and say, "Just a little while longer until we go." You could also ask to go and take a little walk. Maybe we could go and get a drink of water so your body has a chance to get the squirmies out."

Example → (playing with brother/sister/friend who's knocking down the building he's constructing) "I noticed that (person) is trying to bug you. What could you do to help yourself?" If he comes up with a solution (like moving away, getting his brother/sister/friend another toy to play with), praise him and prompt him to do it. If he has a difficult time coming up with ideas, describe what you see, "Well, it looks to me like (person) wants your attention. Do you want to stop building and see what could you do to help him?" If he can't come up with ways to help, ask him, "If you want to keep building, can you think of something else he could do or could s/he help you?"

Self-Regulation of breathing

Stage 1 – I can do it!

The goal of these activities is to help your child learn that he can use slowed breathing (Turtle Breathing) to calm and center himself. Turtle Breathing helps focus his attention on the present moment, not on what might or might not happen. It can reduce his anxiety level and open his mind and body to other possibilities and to learning. The state of calm and being in the 'here and now' gives your child a chance to clear his mind. He can then make greater sense of things happening around him.

Many children, especially those who are quite anxious, have no idea what it feels like to be calm – they spend most of their lives tense and anxious. By helping your child feel what calmness is like, we can help him enjoy that experience and figure out how his body signals rising stress. It might be in his neck or shoulders or tummy - it's very individual. If he can learn the early warning signs, he can help himself before erupting in anger or tears. This is a life-skill that will help your child through to adulthood.

The main executive functions practiced at this stage are:

- inhibitory control – he has to regulate his breathing and focus solely only on it

- self-monitoring – checking to make sure he's using his Turtle Breathing

> **Language of spark***
> ....
> Introduce the activity with "Let's .." This emphasizes shared particip-ipation.
>
> Give meaning, purpose and feelings of comp-etence by telling your child, "Turtle Breathing helps our brains and our bodies feel calm and work better."

ACTIVITIES

For Stage 1, introduce and practice self-regulation in a place that is quiet and relatively calm. Practice at bedtime or when you child is in the bathtub. Check the list of calm places you wrote on page 24.

Tell your child that, now he knows how to tell his body what to do, you are both going to learn how to do slow

Turtle Breathing. Explain, "Turtle Breathing is slow like a turtle. Take a few slow breaths and feel the air come in and out of your nose/mouth. This lets your brain and your body feel calm and quiet." Practice every day – the more often the better – make sure to pick quiet, calm places. At each practice, breathe in and out slowly up to five or six times.

Example ➡ (sitting cross-legged or lying down on the floor in a quiet place with no distractions) Introduce the idea of Turtle Breathing. Say in a calm, quiet voice, "We're going to sit very quietly and still. We breathe in through our noses really slowly, feeling the air go in our noses (hold for a count of two) and then let the air out slowly. Feel the air come out of your nose. This is Turtle Breathing. It helps our brains and our bodies feel calm and work better. Let's do it three times in a row really slowly. Feel the air come in and out of your nose. Do you feel your body become calm? It's nice to feel our breathing and to feel our calm bodies and brains. Can you feel the air in your nose? We're breathing slowly like a turtle and helping our brains and our bodies be calm. Even if our bodies move a little bit, we can still think only about the air coming in and out of our noses."

Stage 2 – I can do it here and here

The goal of this stage is to help your child understand where and when to use his Turtle Breathing to calm and center himself. The main executive functions focused on at this stage are:

- inhibitory control – stopping to do some Turtle Breathing and then regulating his rate of breathing

- planning and organization - thinking ahead to where and when he can use his Turtle Breathing

- working memory - comparing when to use his Turtle Breathing and how it feels to be calm

- cognitive flexibility - doing Turtle Breathing when he needs it

ILLUSTRATION – seven year old boy (Jack) - continued

Jack's mom wonders how in heaven's name she's going to get him to try Turtle Breathing. She understands that Turtle Breathing can help him calm and centre himself but how do you get him to try it out?

There are a couple of ways you might go with this:

1. refer to Turtle Breathing as Darth Vader breathing or some other character he might think is more 'cool'

2. tell him that calming and centering his body will help him play sports or games better because he'll be able to use his brain better. You probably could find some athlete in his favorite sport who uses mindful breathing to help his game. Examples are Kobe Bryant, LeBron James and Michael Jordan (basketball), Derek Jeter (baseball) and Ricky Williams (American football).

Always remember to explain why you and your child need to practice things. Everything needs to have meaning and purpose that makes sense to both you and your child.

ILLUSTRATION – four year old girl (Emma) - continued

Emma's mom thinks this is a great idea. Emma is a pretty busy little girl. Mom's not sure how to get Emma to try Turtle Breathing.

There are a couple of ways you might go with this:

1. Emma really likes animals so breathing slowly like a turtle could really capture her imagination

2. Now you have to give it some meaning and purpose for her. We know Emma loves anything to do with animals so Mom could tell her that mother animals teach their babies how to calm and centre their brains and bodies. She could pretend to be a mother horse or any animal of her choosing and teach her babies how to do Turtle Breathing.

ACTIVITIES

Talk to your child about when he can use his Turtle Breathing to help calm his brain and body and help them work better. Identify some situations that might help him sleep, play or think better. After he's made some suggestions, add situations that may have some emotion attached to them (for example, when he gets really excited about going to his favorite restaurant or feels angry if another child takes over his activity).

Example "I'm thinking about when I can use my Turtle Breathing to make my body and brain calm and work better. How about when I need to think really hard? Would that be a good time to use Turtle Breathing?" Act out the situation. Let your child take a turn preparing himself for doing a challenging activity.

Introduce storybooks with characters feeling different emotions (like the raccoon in *The Kissing Hand* or *The Little Old Lady Who Was Not Afraid of Anything*). Discuss these characters and how they could use Turtle Breathing to help them calm down and think better. Practice Turtle Breathing while pretending to be these characters. Suggestions for different storybooks are in the resources on the Self-regulation Everyday website (www.self-reg-everyday.com).

You and your child can make a little storybook or video that shows him using his Turtle Breathing in situations. Draw pictures or make a video of him using his Turtle Breathing before doing a difficult task or at bedtime when he's trying to get to sleep. Storybooks and videos let him remind himself of the skills over and over again.

At home or out in the community with your child, remind him when Turtle Breathing could help. You can point out someone who's having difficulty controlling themselves and ask your child what the person could do to help himself (do some Turtle Breathing). Remind him about your discussions and storybook characters you read about.

You can also put little turtle stickers in different locations around the house and in the car to remind all family

Language of spark*

Understanding meaning and purpose is encouraged by asking, "Why do you think it's a good idea to use your Turtle Breathing?"

Prompt him to think on his own by asking questions like, "How can you help yourself remember?"

members. The turtle symbolizes the need to stop and check your body and use Turtle Breathing to calm and center yourself. Everyone in the family can practice and use Turtle Breathing.

Stage 3 – I can do it even when ...

The goal of this stage is to help your child cope in different situations by using Turtle Breathing. The main executive functions focused on at this stage are:

- inhibitory control – using Turtle Breathing in order to remain calm even in distracting or stressful situations

- working memory - remembering that he can use his Turtle Breathing if/when he finds himself feeling tense or stressed

- self-monitoring - checking to make sure he's keeping his body and brain calm and using Turtle Breathing when needed

- cognitive flexibility - changing from a state of upset or high activity to calmness using Turtle Breathing

ACTIVITIES

Now that your child has practiced Turtle Breathing and understands why and where it can help him, it's time to bring it into everyday life. Before going about your day talk with him about how he can control his body and how Turtle Breathing can make it even easier. Practice a few Turtle Breaths with your child and move on with your day.

Don't forget to practice Turtle Breathing when your child needs to help calm himself, like at bedtime or before doing homework.

> **Example**

(in the grocery store line-up your child is becoming restless) Engage your child in Turtle Breathing. Be sure to catch your child before he becomes too restless. If he's emotional and tired, he'll have a harder time using Turtle

Breathing. As early as possible, say, "It looks like your brain and your body are having a hard time standing in line. It's hard for me too. Why don't we do some Turtle Breathing to help our brains and bodies stay calm?"

Example ▷ (you're talking to another adult and your child wants you to leave) Again, don't wait too long you talk to him. Comment, "I need to talk to (person) for two more minutes. What could you do to help your body and your brain stay calm?" It generally helps children to tell them exactly how many more minutes you need and stick with that amount of time.

Stage 4 – I can help myself by ...

Move on to this stage when your child shows he can use Turtle Breathing to calm and center himself most of the time. He doesn't have to use it every time he should – it'll take time to become more aware of when he needs to use it. Continue practicing like you did in Stage 1, especially at bedtime or before starting a difficult task.

The goal of this stage is to help your child self-regulate, using his Turtle Breathing in everyday situations and then advocating for himself when needed. The main executive functions focused on at this stage are:

- inhibitory control – calming himself in spite of varying distractions and temptations

- planning and organization – calming himself and thinking ahead to how he might self-advocate

- working memory – thinking about when to use his Turtle Breathing and when to self-advocate in order to help him remain calm

- self-monitoring - checking to see how calm his brain and body are

- cognitive flexibility - changing his state to one of calmness using Turtle Breathing and/or self-advocating to help him remain calm

Language of spark*
....
Help your child develop a sense of control by accepting his ideas – "If you don't want to do Turtle Breathing here, how about you do it over there?"

Give your child lots of opport-unities to demon-strate his new skills. Stand back, getting involved and helping him only when nec-essary.

57

ACTIVITIES

Now it's time for your child to take over more control. Go to places you normally go (dentist, doctor, shopping mall, grocery stores, places of worship, community centers). Be ready to help him think of ways to help himself if he's having difficulty staying calm. You can help him learn some negotiation skills. He could say, "How about ...?", suggesting different ways to help himself. Discuss possible options with him before going into a situation. He may want to leave some places but that's not an option. Quietly doing some Turtle Breathing and closing his eyes and covering his ears may be appropriate.

Example (a group activity is becoming too chaotic and out of control) Talk with your child the moment you see he's becoming upset by what's going on. Quietly comment, "It looks like you're having a hard time here. What could you do to help yourself?" He may decide to practice Turtle Breathing or he may want to leave the situation. Promote Turtle Breathing – he may be more willing to use it on the sidelines rather than right in the middle of the group.

Example (at the dentist's office where he typically is anxious) Practice beforehand some things he can do. Turtle Breathing will help calm him but, if he's having a difficult time staying calm, ask him what things he could do. Leaving isn't an option but he could ask for a short break, a drink of water or his favourite music. Be sure to let the dentist and staff know about these things so they can respond appropriately and positively.

Self-Regulation of the voice

Stage 1 – I can do it!

The goal of the activities is to help your child learn to control the loudness of his voice. The main executive functions practiced at this stage are:

- inhibitory control - he has to control loudness, moving from quiet to normal speaking volume to loud

- self-monitoring – he checks to makes sure his voice is at the volume it should be

For Stage 1, introduce and practice self-regulation in activities your child enjoys. Check back to page 26 where you identified your child's likes and dislikes. Songs and rhymes are naturals for practicing voice control.

Practice in a place that's suitable for loud and quiet voices – it can get raucous! Do it in the car when driving, in the bathtub, or just about anywhere it's okay to be a little noisy.

Check back to page 26

ACTIVITIES

Tell your child that sometimes you can say things really loudly and sometimes quietly. Ask him which way he wants to do a song, rhyme or conversation: loudly, softly or in between. Let him decide and sing or talk at that intensity. Part way through, change the intensity. Take turns with your child so he can decide the intensity. Mix in some changes of speed as well – it's difficult to sign quickly and quietly at the same time, the natural tendency is to get louder.

It may help to have a visual guide for voice loudness. A simple colored dial like the one to the right can help him understand variations in loudness more clearly - green is quiet, yellow is an 'everyday' loudness and/or getting louder, and red is loud. Use the dial to practice and then it can be used later to cue him if his voice is too loud or too quiet. There are a number of apps you can use also – check the Self-regulation Everyday website for a list.

Language of spark*

Introduce the activity with "Let's .." or "How about we ...?" These emphasize shared participation.

Give feelings of competence by telling your child, "You really know how to control your voice."

Increase your child's sense of control by letting him decide the loudness level you both should use.

Example (in the bathtub) "Let's sing (your choice of song). Are you ready?" Sing one round with your child. "How about we do that again but do it really loudly?" (turn the hand

ILLUSTRATION – seven year old boy (Jack) - continued

Jack would love this activity but his mom's concerned that he might not quieten down again. Sometimes, he gets wound up and just keeps going with it.

The trick here will be to have him practice on the quieter side first, before he can become wound up. Jack and his mom should practice whispering conversation between them, alternating with 'in-between' (normal conversation loudness). Once he's in solid control of his loudness, move on to songs that he enjoys or practice in conversation. Start with fairly neutral songs or conversation topics that aren't too exciting. Then introduce songs and topics that have some energy to them – the ones that feel good sung at the top of your lungs or topics of conversation he's passionate about (like who's the best hockey or lacrosse player). Alternate loud, quiet and in-between having Jack decide the loudness level. That puts him in control of the activity which should help him control his voice as well.

To really challenge him and build his resilience, do exciting activities, like competitive games, with Jack deciding if a segment will be done using a quiet, loud or in-between voice – regardless of what happens or how exciting it gets. This is a great challenge and can be fun to see who forgets to use the chosen loudness level first. Make a game of it.

ILLUSTRATION – four year old girl (Emma) – continued

Emma has a tendency to be too quiet, especially in new places or when she's around new people.

The first and most important thing to do is make sure no one (NO ONE!) ever calls her 'shy'. That can be embarrassing for Emma and you could lose her cooperation. It's fine to tell people that it takes time for Emma to warm up to new settings and new people. Make sure people just welcome her and leave her alone for a while. She needs time to look and listen before she's willing to join in.

Talk to Emma directly about how it seems that she needs time to get used to new places and people and it's okay – lots of kids need that. Tell her you know that she likes to check things out first but ask how you could help her. Suggest maybe you and she could talk about who the people will be and what's going to happen before you get to the situation. If she likes that idea, it may help her warm up more quickly. See if she has any suggestions for helping her feel more comfortable.

Next, talk to her about how other people might not understand why she doesn't talk to them. They might think she doesn't like them (some early work on empathy) or maybe she can't talk – this last suggestion should get her interested. Suggest that she just say "Hi" and that will make them feel better and not worry that she can't talk or doesn't like them. Practice this with Emma, making up pretend situations and trading places so you can pretend to be Emma. She might enjoy using puppets, stuffed animals, or animal figures to act out the roles of Emma and Mom.

on the voice meter dial to red or set up the app) Sing it again. "Okay, let's do the next part really softly or quietly. Are you ready?" Sing the next round. "Wow, you really controlled your voice and told it what to do. Well done! (OR "It looks like you have to tell your voice to do what you want. Let's tell it now, voice, you need to sing softly.") Now, how do you want to do the next one, quietly, loudly or in between?"

Sing or talk using the loudness your child chose. "Nice job! You really told your voice what to do. (OR "Keep working. That silly voice needs to listen better. You tell it.) Okay, let's do one more round. How should we do it this time?" After the next round, ask "How did your voice do this time?" If his judgement was accurate, praise him. If it wasn't very well done, say, "Hmm, it didn't sound like the best you can do. Let's do it again and really watch how loud your voice is."

Stage 2 – I can do it here and here

The goal of this stage is to help your child understand where and when he can use different levels of loudness. The main executive functions focused on at this stage are:

- inhibitory control – regulating the loudness of his voice, using a quiet, in between or loud voice when appropriate and switching among them

- planning and organization - thinking ahead to how loud his voice should be in different places

- working memory – recalling the appropriate loudness for different settings

- self-monitoring – checking to make sure his voice is at the right loudness level

- cognitive flexibility - changing the loudness of his voice in different situations

---

Language of spark⁎

Thinking on his own is encouraged by asking, "Why do you think that's a good/not so good idea?" and "How can you help yourself remember?"

Help your child feel competent by saying, "Good thinking!", "How did you know what to do?"

Help him understand the meaning and purpose – "If we use a quiet voice, other people can hear, think, sleep. When we're at a game, it's okay to use a loud voice because we're excited.

ACTIVITIES

Talk to your child about when he should use a loud voice, quiet or in between voice. Think of places and situations at home and in the community where he would need to change loudness (library, sports arena, grandma's house, hospital, playground).

Example

"I'm thinking about how we need to use different voices in different places. How about if (person) is having a nap or is talking on the phone? What should we tell our voice to do?" Act out the situation as needed. Let your child take a turn being the sleeping person. Talk or sing in a really loud voice. Then ask him, "Hmm, do you think that's a good idea? What should I tell my voice?" If he chooses telling his voice to be quiet, praise him for such good thinking. (If he's not sure, act out a scene with him pretending to sleep or talk on the phone and you talking or singing really loudly. Ask, "Is it easy to sleep/talk when I'm making so much noise? It's really hard, isn't it? We need to tell our voice to be quiet.") How can you help yourself remember to use a quiet voice when someone's sleeping or talking on the phone?" Accept his suggestions and add some of your own. Go to other places, some where he can use a loud voice (like the playground) and some where he needs to use a quiet voice (for example, a place of worship, the library).

Introduce storybooks with characters using appropriate and inappropriate voices (like Mortimer in *Mortimer be quiet*). Discuss these characters and their choices about their voices and why and where it's appropriate. Suggestions for different storybooks are in the resources on the Self-regulation Everyday website (www.self-reg-everyday.com).

You and your child can put together a storybook or video that shows him using his voice in ways appropriate to different settings. Draw pictures or make a video of him using a quiet voice when someone is sleeping, a loud voice in the playground, or an in between voice at school or preschool. Your child can review his new skills

Language of spark*

Remembering the meaning and purpose and thinking on his own are encouraged by asking, "Why do you think that's a good/not so good voice to use?"

Help him think on his own by asking, "What should you tell your voice?" and "How can we help ourselves remember?"

on his own this way. This is a great way to let your child review the things he's learned.

Both at home and in the community, comment how your child is controlling his voice in appropriate ways. Remind him about your discussions and about storybook characters.

Stage 3 – I can do it even when ...

The goal of this stage is to help your child cope in situations that might challenge the self-regulation of his voice. The main executive functions focused on at this stage are:

- inhibitory control – regulating the loudness of his voice regardless of what's happening around him

- planning and organization – thinking ahead to choose loudness appropriate to different situations

- working memory - remembering when and where he should use loud, quiet, and in between voices

- self-monitoring - checking to make sure he's controlling his voice appropriately

- cognitive flexibility - changing loudness of his voice for different situations

ACTIVITIES

Now that your child has practiced different voice volumes and understands why and where his voice should be quiet, loud or in between, it's time to practice in everyday life. Go places that are challenging for your child as well as places he can use a loud voice. Before going into situations that are more challenging, talk to him about controlling his voice. Say, "We're going to the library and you remember how our voices are supposed to be there. What could we tell our voices in the library?"

Example (going to a place of worship) If he starts to use a loud voice, ask, "What do you need to tell your voice when we're in church?" If he's unsure, remind him that you talked about using a quiet voice even though some people are allowed to talk loudly. Ask him again, "What do you need to tell your voice?" When he uses a quiet voice, be sure to praise him for remembering. Explain that it makes it easier for other people to hear when he uses a quiet voice.

Stage 4 – I can help myself by ...

Move on to this stage when your child shows he can control his voice most of the time. He doesn't have to have perfect control but he's showing progress. Continue practicing like you did in Stage 1 whenever you can – it's fun and good reminders for everyone.

The goal of this stage is to help your child self-regulate in different settings by advocating for himself. The main executive functions focused on at this stage are:

- inhibitory control – control the loudness of his voice even with distractions, excitement and temptations

- planning and organization - thinking ahead to how the loudness of his voice should be in different situations

- working memory - comparing the present situation to rules about how quiet or loud his voice should be

- self-monitoring - checking to see if his voice is the right loudness for the setting

- cognitive flexibility - changing the loudness of his voice for different situations and/or advocating for himself so he can remain self-regulated

Language of spark*
....
Help your child develop a sense of control by prompting him to make his own decisions about what to do – "What could you do to help yourself?"

Give him opportunities to demonstrate his new skills. Stand back, getting involved only if necessary.

ACTIVITIES

Now that your child has practiced self-regulation of his voice in different places with your support, it's time for him to take over more control. Go places you normally go in the course of family life. Be ready to prompt him to think of ways to help himself if he's having a difficult time controlling his voice.

Example → (a group activity where your child is becoming loud and/or other people are loud and that bothers him) Watch your child closely and look for signs of distress. If he doesn't make some decisions on his own about using a quieter voice or asking others to use quieter voices, talk to him privately and say, "It looks like you're having a hard time here. What could you do to help yourself?" He may decide to practice Turtle Breathing and then use a quieter voice. He may choose to ask another child to use a quieter voice or he may want to leave the situation. Help him decide which choice is most appropriate and which might be best for him.

Refining body self-regulation

Yoga

Yoga is a wonderful way to practice regulating the speed, location and intensity of body movement coordinated with Turtle Breathing. It also helps to improve imitation skills, concentration, body strength, and flexibility. Yoga also doesn't require any exotic equipment or clothing, is simple to learn, and can be done just about anywhere.

First, find a quiet place where you won't be interrupted. The space should be as uncluttered as possible – a place where distractions are minimal. Wear comfortable clothes and use a non-slip mat, if available.

Next, decide what poses you want to use. It's usually best to do a little warm-up first. Do some Turtle Breathing with your child and then demonstrate a pose - help him do it if necessary. Start with a set of positions that (a) feel comfortable for you and your child and (b) let you breathe freely. Remember, the warming up and cooling down parts of yoga are supposed to be gentle and calming.

Simple "corpse" pose		**Calming**
"Child" pose (also called "let's see if you can touch your nose to your knees)		
"Calm heart" pose		
Calming pose "seated forward bend" pose (also known as "Let's see if you can smell your toes")		
Simple "mountain" pose		**Alerting**
"Warrior" pose (also called "Let's see if you can touch the ceiling)		
"Cat" pose		
"Dog", "downward dog" pose		

Some positions are easy for everyone. Have a look at the chart on the next page. Two are labeled "simple" because they require little to no coordination, yet, when coupled with Turtle Breathing, promote a state of calm. Some poses are more calming and quieting. Others are more alerting. You'll notice poses in the table that are labeled "calming"; those are positions that curl the body. The poses labeled "alerting" are ones where the body is stretched. These tend to wake up your muscles and brain.

When you go into a pose, move slowly and be sure to use your Turtle Breathing. If you're going to do a sequence of poses, use the mountain pose between other positions. Start with mountain pose, move slowly into the next pose, and then move back to the mountain pose again before taking on another one. The simple 'corpse' position is an excellent calm place to end your yoga session.

There are a number of resources on the internet, in the library and in stores that can help you. Please check the Self-regulation Everyday website (www.self-reg-everyday.com) for suggestions.

Active games

There are many games and sports that can help you and your child practice body self-regulation. Check the resources on the Self-regulation Everyday website (www.self-reg-everyday.com) for suggestions suitable for children from two to eight years of age.

You can vary games and sports in terms of how quickly or slowly you play them. You can also pretend to be different animals while playing the sport or game (for example, stomping dinosaurs when playing tag). You can play games or sports silently – that would really test voice self-regulation.

There are a lot of stop-and-go games, like freeze tag, *What time is it Mr. Wolf/Fox?*, *Red Light-Green Light*, and *Simon Says*. With those games, you must listen carefully, stop and start your body according to directions.

Household tasks

Living together in a household means everyone helps it run smoothly. Even young children can do household tasks. Being responsible for even simple jobs builds your child's sense of responsibility as well as his self-regulation and independence. You're preparing him to look after himself as he matures and eventually leaves home.

On the next pages are household tasks suitable for different age groups. Two to three year old children can do a few simple tasks on their own. All of the tasks should be done with supervision.

Four to five year olds can do more things than the younger children but still need some help and supervision. Don't expect perfection at first. With a lot of practice, you should see improvement and more independence.

Age appropriate household tasks for children	
2 to 3 year olds	**4 to 5 year olds**
Personal care help brush teeth **Cleaning** help dust throw trash in bin **Meal preparation** put napkins on table put silverware on table **Tidying** help put away toys put books back on shelf **Laundry** put laundry in hamper	**Personal care** help brush teeth wash hands and face select own clothes for the day **Cleaning** help dust throw trash in bin help mop floor help wipe up spills help vacuum **Meal preparation** put napkins on table put silverware on table help clear table **Tidying** help put away toys put books back on shelf help make beds empty silverware & plastic dishes from dishwasher **Laundry** put laundry in hamper **Pet care:** help feed pet

The list of household tasks expands for children between six and eight years of age. Less supervision should be needed also.

Age appropriate household tasks for children	
6 to 7 year olds	**7 to 8 year olds**
Personal care brush teeth help bathe/shower select own clothes for the day	**Personal care** brush teeth brush hair bathe/shower on own select own clothes for the day
Cleaning help dust throw trash in bin help sort recycling help mop floor wipe up spills help vacuum	**Cleaning** dust furniture take out trash help sort recycling mop floor wipe up spills vacuum
Meal preparation set table clear table help carry groceries help put away groceries help make salad	**Meal preparation** set table clear table help with grocery shopping help carry groceries help put away groceries help make salad chop vegetables
Tidying put away toys put books back on shelf help make beds empty dishwasher	**Tidying** put away toys put books back on shelf make bed empty dishwasher
Laundry put laundry in hamper help sort laundry fold laundry	**Laundry** put laundry in hamper help sort laundry fold laundry
Pet care feed pet brush pet	**Pet care** feed pet exercise pet
Yard & garden help rake leaves water plants help plan garden	**Yard & garden** help rake leaves/shovel snow water plants help plan garden clean up pet waste
Family events help plan own birthday party	**Family events** Help plan parties for family members

ILLUSTRATION – seven year old boy (Jack) – continued

There are lots of great active games Jack would enjoy. Try out stop-and-start games, in particular. We know he can rev himself up but we also need to help him calm himself. Try using Turtle Breathing (or whatever you decided to call it) in between so he can experience excitement and calm alternately.

Try your best to get him to do some yoga. You could do it before he does some sport so he can calm and centre himself and get his muscles ready. Also look on the internet for sports stars who practice yoga.

Getting Jack to do household tasks is probably going to be challenging. He's more used to disorganising things than organizing. You should start with a chore list for everyone in the house – Jack has a strong sense of fairness so he needs to see that everyone is doing their part. You could set out one task per person for each day and then have them choose which one they want to do – roll dice to see who gets to choose first (remember, fairness is important to Jack). It would be best to have him do a task that you could look in on. For example, have him set the table while you're able to see what he's doing in order to make sure he gets it done – just throwing the cutlery on the table isn't enough! You may need to give out stars and rewards to get everyone cooperating with household tasks – remember the old days when you got a weekly allowance for completing a certain number of chores each week?

ILLUSTRATION – four year old girl (Emma) – continued

Emma will probably enjoy yoga, especially if you have some of her favourite classical music playing quietly in the background. Yoga would be a great way to start the day, if you can fit it into the schedule. It will calm and centre her and get her muscles ready for play.

Active games will be so much fun with Emma. She loves this sort of thing but may find it challenging to play stop-and-go games. Keep it fun and show how you have problems sometimes stopping your body. She'll enjoy noticing it.

If you can help Emma feel a sense of control, she'll likely enjoy doing household chores. An important thing will be to put her in charge of one important aspect of life at home. She might be put in charge of setting the table every night. Help her make a diagram of where everything should go, then she'll be able to proceed on her own. She's a girl who'll enjoy the responsibility.

5 Cognitive Self-Regulation

The Cognitive Self-Regulation unit comes after your child has built a solid foundation of body self-regulation. He can calm his body and brain and more easily focus his attention.

In the Cognitive Self-Regulation unit, we want to help your child make the best use of his thinking. Our goals are to help your child:

1. pay attention to key things and ignore things that aren't important at that moment

2. think about what he hears and sees and make sure he understands

3. organize his ideas and explain them to other people in ways they can understand.

In the information that follows, you'll find out more about each goal, where and when you might practice the skills with your child, activities you can do to improve his self-regulation, and resources for practicing.

Remember, you can move from one area to another but still keep practicing past skills.

> Be sure to practicing Turtle Breathing in everyday situations, during yoga practice and while practicing the new cognitive skills.

Practice activities center around everyday situations, like doing a household task, playing with favorite toys, or sharing a book. Special materials are kept to a minimum

– any extras will be on the Self-regulation Everyday website (www.self-reg-everyday.com) and suggested storybooks can be borrowed from your local library.

Order of skills

1. First, you're going to help your child **focus his attention**. We want to make sure he's looking and listening to what's important.

2. Next, you'll help him **figure out what to do just by looking** around him.

3. The next step is **making sure he understands** the information he hears, reads or sees.

4. The last area you'll work on is helping your child organize his ideas so he can **explain his thoughts and ideas** in ways that others can understand.

NOTE: The cognitive activities in this unit are quite advanced for many children. **DO NOT expect children under five to do all of them on their own.** Some of the charts will show you what to expect at different age levels.

Your child will need your support, encouragement, and patience. You'll see improvement if you continue to practice and model these skills.

Accept as your child's present level whatever he's doing within your practice session. Write down what he did (and the date) and strive for a little bit more each practice session. Having a record will help you appreciate the gains your child makes.

Self-Regulation of attention

Attention span increases with age in children. Use the estimates for activity length (from page 33) as reasonable length for concentrated attention in two to eight year olds.

If your child is	Approximate attention span
2 to 3 years of age	4 to 6 minutes
3 to 4 years of age	6 to 8 minutes
4 to 5 years of age	8 to 10 minutes
5 to 6 years of age	10 to 12 minutes
6 to 8 years of age	12 to 14 minutes

If your child can easily pay attention for fewer than the number of minutes for his age level and starts getting restless, work with that amount of time **regardless of his age**. That's his current attention span. As you practice with him, try to keep him engaged in an activity for a little bit more each time, then stop the activity. Always end on a positive note. Slowly edge up the time but don't necessarily expect him to be at the top level for his age group right away. Two good minutes is always better than struggling through five.

Stage 1 – I can do it!

The goal of these activities is to help your child focus his attention. Learning to direct his attention to important things and ignore other things will make life easier. We'll work systematically, doing one thing at a time. This will help him focus and he'll be less likely to miss important details. Once your child shows he can be systematic and can stay on track, multi-tasking can be introduced. Let's make sure his 'one-thing-at-a-time' foundation is solid first.

The main executive functions practiced at this stage are:

- inhibitory control - making sure he works systematically and doesn't miss anything

- planning and organization – working system-

Language of spark*
....
Introduce the activity with "Let's .." or "How about we ...?" These emphasize shared partici-pation.

Give meaning and purpose to the skill by defining it and explaining why you use it, "We're going to be really systematic. That means we do one thing at a time so we don't miss anything."

Increase his sense of control by suggesting you and he use your 'finder fingers' to help your brains focus.

atically and doing one thing at a time

- self-monitoring - checking to make sure he's on track and not missing anything important

ACTIVITIES

Tell your child you're going to practice together on "being **systematic**". That means we're going to do one thing at a time so we don't miss anything." Check back to your list of things he likes on page 26 and use activities that incorporate some of them. Practice is much more fun when it centers around things he likes.

If he's looking at something and having difficulty being systematic, suggest he use his "finder finger" (his index finger) to help keep track and avoid becoming overwhelmed. Help him move his finder finger from one item to the next, left to right and top to bottom (just like in reading).

For children who seem overwhelmed by busy, detailed pictures or activities, cover some of it up. You and your child can use sticky notes or blank pieces of paper to put on things that he finds distracting. Explain to him, "Covering things up can help our brains if there's too much stuff to look at." If the activity continues to be distracting even when you cover up some of the information, go to a simpler activity.

Play card and board games that emphasize systematic search, like *Concentration*, and/or follow a specific sequence of actions. Check the Resources files on the Self-regulation in Everyday Life website for suggested materials and resources suitable for children from two to eight year of age.

Example ➡ (setting the dinner table) "Let's be really systematic putting the cutlery out. We'll do one thing at a time so we don't miss anything. How about we put out all the knives first (or, set one place at a time)? How many do we need?" Then ask, "What should be put out next? How many do we need again?" and so on until everything is in place.

ILLUSTRATION – seven year old boy (Jack) – continued

Jack gets really frustrated when he is prompted to work systematically. He's used to just diving into things and getting them done. What's this slowing down stuff about??

You're going to have to prove to him that it's worth his while. He likes Lego™ so that may be a place to start. You could ask him to complete a new model while timing him – hopefully, he'll run into problems with missing pieces or pieces in the wrong order. Try the same model or a new one but use a systematic approach (get all the pieces you need and then start at the bottom and work up). If you use the same model, he probably won't notice that practice alone helps him go faster. Be sure to time him. Compare the times with him. The numbers should help convince him.

Have other people important to Jack explain why they do things systematically.

A good example for him would be to put on his sports equipment any old order. You could help him put his shoes on and then try to put on shorts and socks – yes, socks over top of his shoes! Draw in his favorite sports and sports heroes wherever you can. They just might convince him that systematic is a good way to go.

Be sure to emphasize working systematically when he does his homework.

ILLUSTRATION – four year old girl (Emma) – continued

Emma's generally a pretty busy little person who finishes things quickly. She'll likely struggle with slowing down. Be sure to use Turtle Breathing to help her calm her brain and body before practicing.

Help Emma understand that doing one thing at a time helps her brain work better and she's less likely to miss something important. Tell her that's how big kids who go to school do things – she likes to think of herself as being grown up and ready for school.

Try Emma out with getting dressed in any old order. It'll help her see how important it can be to do one thing at a time. She'd also find it funny to try to put her socks over her shoes or underpants over her jeans.

Let her teach her animals how to be systematic. She can act out scenarios with them (like feeding them or putting on equipment) and teach them how to do one thing at a time. That'll give her a sense of control and improve her use of a systematic approach.

Example (looking at a *Where's Waldo/Wally?* book) "Let's find him. How about we do it systematically so we don't miss any? We could use your finder finger (index finger) to help our eyes look really carefully. We could also look for just one color – what would that be? Let's give it a go." You could also suggest that he cover up the parts of each page he already examine - "So it's easier for your brain."

Stage 2 – I can do it here and here

Move on to this stage when your child shows that he can work systematically and do one thing at a time for most activities.

The goal of this stage is to help your child understand where and when he should be systematic and focus his attention. The main executive functions practiced at this stage are:

- inhibitory control - making sure he doesn't miss anything important

- planning and organization - being systematic, looking at one thing at a time

- working memory – keeping the goal in mind as he goes through the task systematically

- self-monitoring - checking to make sure he's on track and looking for the important things

- cognitive flexibility - changing his approach to activities if needed

ACTIVITIES

Talk to your child about when he should be systematic and do just one thing at a time and when he doesn't have to worry about being systematic. Think of all sorts of places and situations at home and in the community – when completing puzzles, doing household tasks, looking for misplaced things around the house, doing homework, doing crafts, dressing, getting ready for bed.

Example

"I'm thinking about when we need to do one thing at a time and be systematic. How about when we're raking leaves (shoveling snow, sweeping or vacuuming – whatever your child has experience with)? Should we just go all over the place and do a little bit here and a little bit there?" Act out the situation as needed. Exaggerate hopping from place to place. Let your child take a turn. Then ask, "Do you think that would be a good idea? What should we do?" If he chooses to remind his brain and body to work systematically, praise him for such good thinking. If he's not sure, pretend to read a book but flip from back to front and not from page to page. Ask, "Is that a good idea? Would I know what the book's about if I just looked at a few pages? That would make it really difficult, wouldn't it? We need to tell our brain and our body to go systematically and look at one page at a time. How can you help yourself remember to be systematic and do one thing at a time?" Accept just about any suggestion your child makes. You can also make suggestions about things you might use to remind yourself. Go to other examples where he should be systematic (like when printing or writing, playing on the computer, putting on his clothes, taking a bath, cooking).

You and your child can create a little storybook or video that shows him being systematic in different settings. Draw pictures or make a video of him putting together a toy (like Lego™ action figures) that have a certain order for each piece. Do a household task, like mopping, that needs to be done systematically so no spots or spills are missed. Storybooks and videos can be reviewed again and again by you and your child.

At home or out in the community with your child, comment how he's doing one thing at a time. Share that you sometimes forget to be systematic and do one thing at a time. Let him catch you forgetting so he can remind you what to do. We want him to realize that we all need to remind ourselves from time to time.

Language of spark*

Understanding meaning and purpose and thinking on his own are encouraged by asking, "Why do you think that's a good/not so good idea?"

Prompt him to think on his own by asking questions like, "What should you tell your brain and your body?" and "How can we help ourselves remember?"

Stage 3 – I can do it even when ...

Move on to this stage after your child shows that he understands he can work systematically and do one thing at a time in different places and with different activities. He knows where and when to tell his brain and his body to be systematic.

The goal of this stage is to help your child cope in situations that might challenge his new systematic ways. The main executive functions focused on at this stage are:

- inhibitory control – working systematically even with temptations and distractions

- planning and organization – doing one thing at a time and thinking ahead

- self-monitoring - checking to see how he's doing and not allowing unimportant things to distract him

- cognitive flexibility – changing his approach in different situations

ACTIVITIES

Now that your child has practiced and understands why and where the skills are important, we need to give him one more tool. He needs to learn that he can purposely **ignore** things that aren't important. Before using everyday situations, explain, "If something's bugging/bothering you, you can just ignore it." Ask him to do something that might distract you, like singing loudly or dancing around, while you're reading a book. Show him how you can still continue what you're doing. Tell him, "I can just ignore you so that doesn't bother me." Get your child to do some activity while you try to distract him. Continue practicing and keep it fun and playful.

Go places where he's had difficulty regulating himself in the past. Make sure you expose him to challenges that

Language of spark*
....
Prompt your child to think on his own with comments like, "You really told your brain and your body what to do. What did you tell them?" Model statements like, "Brain, we need to do one thing at a time and just ignore that other stuff."

Help your child feel competent with statements like, "Good thinking!", "You really know how to tell your brain and your body what to do." and "Look at how you just ignored that. Well done!"

aren't too difficult but that provide him with chances to practice his new skills.

Example ▷ (your child is working hard at his favorite computer game and his younger sibling is trying to take over the game) Comment, "Wow, look at how you are ignoring (person) and continuing to play your game systematically. You are so clever. You're making it easier for your brain and your body by ignoring (person). Good for you!" If the younger sibling doesn't stop trying to take over, you might prompt him to leave his brother/sister alone. This is a chance to model how to use Turtle Breathing to stay calm and suggest the other child do something else (a little social problem-solving).

Example ▷ (your child is reading quietly and someone turns on the television, he looks bothered by the noise) Ask, "Is the TV making it hard for you to concentrate? What could you tell your brain?" If he seems unsure, remind him about ignoring things that bug you. Ask, "Could that help you right now? Tell your brain what to do."

Stage 4 – I can help myself by ...

Move on to this stage when your child shows he can work systematically, do one thing at a time, and ignore distractions most of the time.

The goal of this stage is to help your child to support his own self-regulation in different settings by advocating for himself. The main executive functions are:

- inhibitory control - working systematically and ignoring temptations and distractions

- planning and organization - doing one thing at a time and thinking ahead

- working memory - comparing the present situation to what he needs in order to work optimally

- self-monitoring - checking to see how he's doing and ignoring unimportant things and figuring out when he needs to change in order to continue

- cognitive flexibility – changing his approach in different situations and advocating for himself if needed

ACTIVITIES

Now that your child has practiced working systematically and ignoring things that interfere with his concentration and attention, it's time for him to help himself. Go to busy places where he's involved in activities. Be ready to prompt him to think of ways to help himself if he's having a difficult time controlling his attention and focus. Ideas that your child thinks of will usually stick with him more than ones you suggest.

Example (doing school work or a craft) Watch your child. The moment you notice he's having difficulty working systematically, comment, "It looks like your brain and your body are having a hard time doing things in order and doing one thing at a time. What could you do to help yourself?" If he comes up with an idea, praise him. If he has a difficult time coming up with an idea, say, "You know when I have a hard time concentrating and doing one thing at a time, I take a Turtle Breath and then tell my brain, "Remember, brain, it's better to do one thing at a time and to work systematically. Then I won't miss anything," If he continues to have a difficult

> ### Language of spark*
> ....
> Prompt your child to think on his own by asking, "What could you do to help yourself?"
>
> Give your child opportunities to demonstrate his new skills. Stand back, getting involved only when necessary.

time, you can suggest he go to a quieter place to do the activity or wear ear protectors if the noise is too loud for him.

Example (getting ready to go outside and someone is trying to make him hurry) If he seems affected by this (for example, forgetting to put his pants on before his shoes or mittens after his boots), say, "I noticed your brain and your body are having a hard time being systematic. What could you do to help yourself?" Remind him to take a Turtle Breath, ignore the distractions, and do one thing at a time. Prompt him to think of ways he can help himself. Suggest asking the other person to be patient and wait a little longer for him to finish what he's doing or going to a quieter place to get himself ready.

Figuring out what to do

Stage 1 – I can do it!

The goal of these activities is to help your child use his new focused attention to look around and figure out what to do. Emphasize looking for **signals**, **clues**, and **models**.

Signals help us know where to go, what to do and what's happening (for example, a red light is a signal that tells us to stop).

Clues are like signals but they're sometimes hidden and difficult to find (for example, crumbs on someone's chin suggest he just ate a cookie, looking for the fellow in the red-striped shirt and glasses in *Where's Waldo/Wally?*).

Models show us what to do (for example, a photo of a cake in a recipe show us what it's supposed to look like when it's done).

The main executive functions practiced at this stage are:

- inhibitory control - making sure he takes the time to look around and doesn't get distracted by things that aren't important

- planning and organization - being systematic and figuring out how to use the signals, clues or models to guide him

- working memory – remembering the signal, clue or model and reminding himself about the most important focus

- self-monitoring - checking to make sure he's on track

- cognitive flexibility - being able to switch between pieces of information and ideas, between the signal, clue or model and his own work

An example of adult use of signals, clues and models is when you want to find a toilet in an unfamiliar restaurant. You look first for signals – where is a sign that says "Toilets" or "Women/Men". If that doesn't work, you look for clues – there's a person talking to a waiter and the waiter's pointing toward a doorway; that's got to be the way to the toilet. Another way to locate the restroom is to look for a customer who seems to be heading toward the back of the restaurant with a sense of purpose.

For Stage 1, introduce and practice self-regulation in everyday activities. Household tasks, crafts and homework work well but be sure incorporate some things he likes (check your list on page 26).

ACTIVITIES

As you're about to begin a task, craft or other activity, ask, "Do you know what to do?" If he describes how he's going to do the task and it's what you had in mind, say, "That's what I was thinking. How did you know that?" Listen to his explanation and highlight his use of signals, clues and/or models. Explain how signals, clues, and models can help:

Language of spark*

Introduce the activity with "Let's .." or "How about we …?" These emphasize shared participation.

Give feelings of competence saying, "You really know how to look for signals/clues/models."

Prompt him to think on his own. Ask him to look for a signal, clue or model that might tell him what to do.

Signals help us know where to go, what to do, and what's happening, just like a red light is a signal that tells us to stop.

Clues are like signals but they're a little sneakier. We have to be like detectives and look carefully for clues about what we're supposed to do.

Models show us what to do or how something's supposed to look. Just like on the boxes for some toys, they show us a picture of what we can build.

Keep in mind that models can also be mental images of past experiences (for example, I remember how we put up that tent before). Increasingly, ask him to make a picture in his brain about how he wants something to look and then to follow that model.

Example ➤ (your child is about to join other children in a group activity) Ask, "What do you think you're supposed to do here?" Wait for his response. Point out the most important signals, clues and/or models: "I noticed everyone's standing in a row. That's a model that tells me what to do." See if he can detect any other features that will guide him in the group activity. Praise him for all attempts. Help direct his attention to all relevant signals, clues, and models. Review the information and then encourage him to join the group.

Example ➤ (cooking or other household task) "Okay, let's think about what we're going to do here. How do you think we should do it?" Once he makes a suggestion, ask him, "How did you know that?" If it was a suggestion that would work, help him highlight the signals, clues or models that helped him figure it out. If his suggestion was likely to lead him in the wrong direction, comment, "That's really interesting but I'm not sure it's going to work. What's an important signal/clue/model that can help us know what to do?" Point out important signals, clues and/or models as needed and explain how they helped you.

ILLUSTRATION – seven year old boy (Jack) – continued

Jack likes the idea of being a detective but he still needs work on taking the time to look for them. His mom includes Turtle Breaths before starting activities to give him a little more time before diving in.

Homework is a perfect place for him to practice his skills. Cover up any written directions and have him become Detective Jack and figure out what he's supposed to do. Then let him read the directions to see if he was right. Review all the signals, clues and models he used and any he missed.

Jack really knows and loves his favorite sports. After he plays a game, ask him how he knew what to do (be sure to tell him you don't really understand the game). This will be a great chance to find out the signals, clues and models he uses to help himself. Also, by having him talk about them, they become more solid in his mind.

ILLUSTRATION – four year old girl (Emma) – continued

Emma seems to use signals, clues and models pretty easily. The question is: is she aware of what she's going? She probably isn't.

It'll help her make more effective use of signals, clues and models now and in the future if they're pointed out and discussed with her. After she's finished an activity, her mom can point out signals, clues and models Emma seemed to use. Sometimes, she can ask Emma which she used. Also, Mom needs to catch her before she starts an activity and ask what she's going to do. Ask, "How do you know that? – being sure to ask in a truly curious (non-testing) way. Emma loves it when Mom tells her how clever she is to notice signals, clues and models.

Stage 2 – I can do it here and here

Move to this stage when your child shows he understands the concepts of signals, clues, and models and can use them to guide his behavior.

The goal of this stage is to help your child understand where and when he should look for signals, clues, and models.

The main executive functions at this stage are:

- inhibitory control – not just leaping into an activity but, instead, looking for signals, clues, and models

- planning and organization – following a plan based on the signals, clues, and models

- working memory – keeping the signal, clue or model in mind while he starts and continues the activity

- self-monitoring - checking to make sure he didn't miss an important signal, clue or model

- cognitive flexibility – looking for different signals, clues and models in different situations

ACTIVITIES

Talk to your child about when it's really important to look for signals, clues, and models. Also, ask him when it's okay just to do something any old way. Practice in places and situations at home and in the community, making sure you get input from your child.

Example "I'm thinking about when we need to look for signals, clues, and models. How about when we're at the movies/cinema? We know we have to buy some tickets. I see a line/queue of people. What signal tells us what to do? When I make a picture in my head, I see a sign that says "Tickets/Box Office". That's a signal telling us where we need to go. Then I see a line/queue of people. I think that's a model for us. That tells us we need to line

> Language of spark*
> ....
> Understanding meaning and purpose is encouraged by asking, "Why do you think that's a good/not so good idea?"
>
> Prompt him to think on his own by asking questions like, "How do you know what to do?"
>
> Help your child feel competent with statements like, "You figured that out all by yourself!", "You're so clever."

up/queue too." Act out the situation as needed. Let your child take a turn pretending to go to the movie theatre – you can even make signs together. Then ask, "How did you know what to do?" Praise him for looking for and identifying at least one signal, clue or model. Pretend you're in other locations familiar to your child. Prompt him to be a detective and find signals, clues, and models that tell him what to do.

Share books like *I Spy* and *Look and Find* series as well as *Where's Waldo/Wally* books to practice looking for signals and clues. Illustrated cookbooks and toy assembly instructions are excellent sources for models.

You and your child can put together a storybook or video that shows him finding signals, clues and models in different settings. Draw a picture or take a video of him looking at pictures of finished models or recipes to help guide him, looking for traffic lights to tell you when to stop and go and seeing if he can find clues to help himself solve a problem.

At home or out in the community, comment about signals, clues, and models you see and what they tell you to do. Have your child look for signals, clues, and models. You'll be surprised how many we use each day. Be sure to make the occasional mistake so your child can correct you.

Stage 3 – I can do it even when ...

Move on to this stage after your child shows he understands that he can look for signals, clues, and models to figure out expectations in different settings.

The goal of this stage is to help your child cope in situations that might challenge his self-regulation and his ability to identify key signals, clues, and models. The main executive functions focused on at this stage are:

- inhibitory control – ignoring distractions and temptations to leap in before looking for important information

- planning and organization - thinking ahead, looking for key information to guide him

- working memory - remembering the signal, clue or model and what he's supposed to do

- self-monitoring - checking to see how he's doing and if he's following his plan or needs to change it

- cognitive flexibility - changing his course of action if his initial plan doesn't work out

ACTIVITIES

Now that your child has practiced these skills and understands why and where they're important, it's time to take them on the road. Go to more challenging places. You can do some preventive work with your child beforehand, talking to him about what he has to remind his body and his brain to do. For example, "What kinds of things can we look for so we can figure out what to do?" (answer: signals, clues, and/or models).

> **Example** (busy shopping center or store) "What are we looking for again? Oh that's right, we're going to look at new shoes for you. What should we look for to help us find the store?" Help your child think of clues, such as landmarks in the form of elevators or other stores that are near the

Language of spark*
....
Prompt your child to think on his own, saying, "You really told your brain what to do. What did you tell it?" Model statements like, "Brain, you need to look really carefully for signals, clues and models that can help us know what to do."

Help your child feel competent with statements like, "Good thinking!", "You really know how to look for signals/clues/ models."

93

shoe store. The mall directory can also serve as a model of the layout which shows where the shoe store is.

Stage 4 – I can help myself by ...

Move on to this stage when your child shows that he can use signals, clues, and models to guide his behavior in important places. He doesn't have notice everyone but he should be making progress.

The goal of this stage is to help your child support his own self-regulation in different settings by advocating for himself. The main executive functions focused on at this stage are:

Language of spark*

Prompt your child to think on his own saying, "You look like you're having a hard time figuring out what to do. What can you do to help yourself?"

Help your child know that there's shared participation by reminding him you'll help if it's needed but he has to use his own brain first.

- inhibitory control – ignoring distractions and temptations to leap in before looking for important information

- planning and organization - thinking ahead, looking for key information and following it

- working memory - remembering the signal, clue or model and what he's supposed to do

- self-monitoring - checking to see how he's doing

- cognitive flexibility – finding ways to advocate for himself so he can continue

ACTIVITIES

Now that your child has practiced self-regulation in different places with your support, it's time for him to take over more control. Be ready to prompt him find ways to help himself if he's having a difficult time figuring out what to do. Be sure he takes the time he needs, takes a Turtle Breath, checks things systematically, and ignores things that aren't important. Remind him he can always ask for help if he needs it. Say, "Asking for help is the smart thing to do but you have to try your best first." If he has a difficult time dealing with the situation, ask him what he can do to help himself. Then take that suggestion and help him think of other alternatives. These are opportunities to build flexibility in problem-solving while remaining calm.

Understanding information

Stage 1 – I can do it!

The goal of the activities is to help your child learn to put together pieces of information he sees and hears and to make sure he understands. It's like taking things you hear and/or see and putting the pieces together like a puzzle.

The main executive functions practiced at this stage are:

- inhibitory control – not leaping at the first piece of information but, instead, listening to it all

- planning and organization – organizing the information into a whole image

- working memory – hanging on to the information, putting pieces together and making sure they make sense

- self-monitoring – checking to make sure put all important pieces together and understands

- cognitive flexibility – being able to change his ideas as he gathers more information

ACTIVITIES

You're going to practice following directions with your child. It's important to keep in mind that the amount and type of information children can understand and remember changes as they mature. Some basic guidelines[26,27] are shown on the next page. They're organized by age group but go to whatever level describes your child best. Then, as he improves, move on to more challenging amounts of information.

We want to help your child listen carefully, think about it, make a picture in his head, say it over to himself, and then do what was requested. His new skills in focusing attention, ignoring distractions and looking for signals, clues, and models will help him. Before giving a

> **Language of spark***
> ....
> Give him a sense of shared participation as well as the need to think on his own, saying, "Let me help you so you know next time".
>
> Help him understand the meaning and purpose by encouraging him to make pictures in his brain and repeat to himself to help him remember.
>
> Give feelings of competence by telling your child, "You really know how to make pictures/a movie in your brain."

direction, help your child understand, "We have to listen really carefully and make a picture (or a movie) in our heads, and then say the important parts to ourselves. That helps us remember what to do." Say a simple two-part direction (for example, "Get a banana and peel it" or "Get your coat and put it on") and model thinking about the words. Repeat the main parts of the direction, then do what the request said. Prompt your child to try the same. If he has difficulty, choose a direction with fewer parts and try again – you can go on to more difficult ones later.

Typical Age Range++	Directions children can remember, understand, and follow
2 to 3 years	Directions with two related parts ("Go to your room and get your shoes.") – for this child, the parts are related because his shoes are kept in his room
3 to 4 years	Directions with two to three related parts ("Go to the playroom, pick up all your toys and come back here.") – the parts are related because the toys are in the playroom.
4 to 5 years	Directions with three to four related parts or two to three unrelated parts ("Touch your nose, run and touch the wall, and say "puppy dog" two times.")
5 to 6 years	Directions with three to four unrelated parts ("Put your pencil on the table, jump three times and sit down")
6 to 8 years	Directions with four to five unrelated parts ** just for reference, adults can remember 5 to 9 pieces of unrelated information
++ some children will develop these skills earlier and some later – the age range in this chart is just an average. Check to see what type and amount of information your child can remember and start there.	

Make sure he says the main parts of the directions over to himself, making a picture in his head, while doing what the direction says. If picturing the direction in his head doesn't seem to make remembering easier, help him pretend to do the actions as he hears the directions. For example, if you tell him to go and pick up his clothes, help him make a 'picking up' action while he listens. Keep it fun and playful. Many children like being 'teacher' so let him give directions to you. It can increase his enthusiasm and participation.

Don't worry about your child's saying the directions out loud to himself. As you practice and he gets better and better, prompt him to say it quietly to himself. Over time, he'll begin to say it in his head.

Check the resources page on the Self-regulation Everyday website for example directions. You can play games like the *Telephone Game or I Packed My Suitcase* (see the resources on the Self-regulation in Everyday Life website for instructions for these and other listening games).

Stage 2 – I can do it here and here

Move to this stage when your child shows that he's successfully following most directions you give him. Keep practicing like you did in Stage 1 whenever you can, keeping it fun for everyone.

The goal of this stage is to help your child understand where and when he should listen carefully to directions.

The main executive functions focused on at this stage are:

- inhibitory control – not just jumping in without thinking about the information he hears

- planning and organization - listening to the information and thinking ahead to what he's going to do once he puts it together

- working memory – hanging on to the parts of the directions, saying them over in his head and putting them together in sequence

- self-monitoring – checking to make sure he understands what was said

- cognitive flexibility - changing how carefully he listens in different situations

Language of spark*

Understanding meaning and purpose is encouraged by explaining, "That helps us remember what to do." and "If we don't listen, we won't know what to do." or "You might miss supper if you forget to listen."

Help your child experience shared participation by giving him a chance to be 'teacher' and give you directions.

ILLUSTRATION – seven year old boy (Jack) – continued

Jack is improving in taking a little more time before diving into things. He needs help with direction-following, however. He often seems to listen to what he wants, ignoring the rest. He should be able to reliably follow directions that contain four to five pieces of information.

If Jack's mom makes sure he knows that making a picture in his brain and saying the directions over to himself is the 'smart' thing to do, he must might buy into it. He also needs to hear that is what just about everyone does it. Jack is the kind of fellow who thinks that, if you have to work too hard at something, maybe you're not 'smart'. He really thinks either you've got it or you don't. It'd like help him to be reminded of how hard he had to work and think when he first learned to ride his bike or play lacrosse and, after lots of practice, it got a lot easier. The same thing happens with following directions – first, you've got to work at it and then it gets easier.

Jack will like the activities that miss out words or use silly or advanced words. He likes being tracked and tricking other people.

ILLUSTRATION – four year old girl (Emma) – continued

Emma's improving in her attention and calm body and brain but her responses to directions could be better. She should be able to follow directions containing four to five pieces of related information (or two to three pieces of unrelated).

She has a bit of an artistic flair so it would be helpful and fun for her to draw pictures of the information she hears. That would slow her down a bit and make sure she's hears all of the details. Emma and her mom can take turns drawing pictures of directions they give to each other. What fun! This'll be a great way to review strategies with Emma (saying directions over to yourself, asking the other person to repeat what they said, etc.) and highlight the need to use them.

ACTIVITIES

Ask your child, "When do we need to listen really carefully and make sure we understand what the people are talking about? When is it okay not to listen too carefully?" Think of places and situations at home and in the community. For example, we need to listen to our parents and teachers and other people in the community. Help him understand important signal words for listening, like when someone says his name or when teacher says, "Now, children ..." or "This is really important." You can make a list of signal words with him. He also needs to know we should ignore kids who are saying mean things or are using swear words, and people who might distract us by their noise or loud talking.

Example "I'm thinking about when we need to listen really carefully and make sure we understand. How about when Dad says something to me? What should I do?" Act out the situation as needed, sometimes ignoring and sometimes paying attention. Prompt your child to add his ideas of when it's important to listen carefully (for example, when he's told it's time for supper, when his teacher talks). Ask him, "Why do you think it's important to listen to (person)?".

You and your child can put together a storybook or video that shows him listening carefully in different settings. For example, draw a picture or make a video of listening, saying a direction over to himself and making a picture in his head at school or preschool, at group activities like sports, or at home. Your child will love reviewing the storybooks and video and that will help refresh his memory.

Stage 3 – I can do it even when ...

Move to this stage once your child shows that he focuses attention and repeats directions over to himself most of the time. He should show that he has some understanding of when he should listen carefully and when he can ignore things that people say.

The goal of this stage is to help your child cope in situations that might challenge his ability to follow directions. The main executive functions focused on at this stage are:

- inhibitory control – not letting distractions and events around him interfere with his listening and understanding

- planning and organization - listening to the information and thinking ahead to what he's going to do

- working memory – hanging on to the parts of the directions, saying them over in his head and putting them together in a sequence and deciding if it makes sense

- self-monitoring – checking to make sure he's listening and understanding

- cognitive flexibility - changing how carefully he listens in different situations

ACTIVITIES

Once your child shows he can listen carefully to directions and can follow them, introduce some challenges. The challenges are in the form of words he can't understand. The main goal is to help him make sure he understands.

Give him a direction just like you did before but, occasionally, add a word or made-up word you know he won't understand. For example, ask him, "Go and get your anorak/snickerdoodle and put it on" – one word is probably unfamiliar to young children and the other is nonsense. Ask him, "Did you say it over in your head to make sure you know what to do?" If he says "Yes", prompt him to do what you said. If he looks unsure, ask him, "Do you know what to do? Do you know what anorak/snickerdoodle is? I was trying to trick you. If you don't understand, you can just say, "What's that? or "What's an anorak/snickerdoodle?" That's the smart thing to do so you make sure you understand."

> **Language of spark***
>
> Prompt your child to think on his own with questions like, "What should you do If you don't understand?
>
> Encourage him to demonstrate his knowledge by stopping you if he doesn't know what to do and ask you to say the direction again or tell him what the word means.
>
> Help your child feel competent, saying, "Good thinking!", "You really know how to listen."
>
> Give your child a sense of control by letting him know he can ask for help if he doesn't understand something.

Practice these challenging directions several times every day. Give your child a chance to make up challenging directions for you so you have to ask him to explain.

Children between two and four years have a harder time with things like this. If your child has a lot of difficulty, use one-part directions and include one silly, nonsensical word in each so they're more obvious.

Now that your child has practiced using strategies to remember directions, he understands why and where it's important to listen, and he knows what to do if he doesn't understand, it's time to take these skills into the community. Go places where listening is important (for example, sports practice, dentist).

Show him how sometimes you don't understand and how you try to figure it out. Say, "I don't know what he said. Did you hear it all? What did he say?" This will show him that everybody has a hard time understanding sometimes. It also shows him that you can ask if you're not sure. Help him understand, in large groups, you can ask the person beside you. At school, you can ask your teacher and, at sports practice, you can ask your coach.

Introduce storybooks with characters who have a difficult time listening. Discuss these characters and what things they could help themselves. Suggestions for different storybooks are in the resources on the Self-regulation Everyday website (www.self-reg-everyday.com).

When you're at home or out in the community, comment about how he's listening carefully. Point out when you forget to listen carefully. Praise him when he asks for someone to repeat or clarify what they said.

Stage 4 – I can help myself by ...

Move on to this stage when your child shows he can pay attention to important directions, ask for help if he's unsure and then carry them out successfully.

The goal of this stage is to help your child support his listening and understanding in different settings by advocating for himself. The main executive functions focused on at this stage are:

- inhibitory control – not letting distractions and events around him interfere with his listening and understanding and keeping himself from proceeding with only partial information

- planning and organization - listening to the information and thinking ahead to what he's going to do if he understands or he doesn't

- working memory – hanging on to the parts of the directions, putting them together and deciding if they make sense

- self-monitoring – checking to make sure he's listening and understanding

- cognitive flexibility - changing how carefully he listens in different situations, being willing to switch his thinking as new information comes along

> Language of spark*
> ....
> Prompt your child to think on his own saying, "What could you do to help yourself?"
>
> Give your child opportunities to demonstrate his new skills. Stand back and get involved only when necessary. It's okay to let him struggle a bit.

ACTIVITIES

Now that your child has practiced paying attention to, checking his understanding of and following directions, it's time for him to take over more control. Give your child directions so he can't hear all of the words. You can cough or sneeze instead of saying one of the key words in a direction or statement. You can also whisper a key word so he can't hear it. If ignores the part he couldn't hear or he tries to follow the direction, stop him and ask, "Are you really sure you understand? I don't think I heard all of the words. I was trying to trick you because you're such a good listener. If you're not sure, all you have to do is say, "Say that again, please." Get him to ask you to say it again and repeat the direction but, this time, make sure all of the direction is clear.

Do this in the community. Be ready to prompt him to think of ways to help himself if he's having a difficult time hearing or understanding directions. First, ask very broad questions like, "What can you do to help yourself?" This is where it gets tricky for both of you – how do you deal with partial information when you're out in public. The ways to find the missing information could include putting up your hand and asking the speaker to clarify, guessing, or asking the person beside you. This is a time to give your child some options that fit best with different situations. Other options can include going closer to the person who's speaking, moving away from interfering noises or asking someone making noise to use a quieter voice.

Example →(your child is listening to you read to him but you're not sure if he's listening and/or understanding) Ask, "Is this story going okay for you?" If he says, "Yes", ask him which part is his favorite. Ask him questions so you get a clearer idea of what he's understanding. If it's clear that he's not hearing all of the important information and/or not putting it together into a clear image, review strategies with him – ignoring distractions, saying it over to himself, making a picture in his head, asking Mom to repeat parts he doesn't understand. It may help him to draw pictures of the story as Mom reads along. That way he'll keep alert and Mom can see where the breakdowns are occurring.

Explaining his thoughts and ideas

Stage 1 – I can do it!

The goal of these activities is to help your child explain his thinking and ideas in ways that other people can understand. We're not going to deal with issues related to how clearly your child speaks – you'd be best to check with a speech-language therapist for help with speech sounds. What we're focusing on is including all important ideas in an organized way. We'll work on describing objects, animals, or people and telling stories so other people can understand them.

The main executive functions practiced at this stage are:

- inhibitory control – not just blurting out ideas

- planning and organization – putting his ideas in a coherent order

- working memory – remembering which information is important to describe and how to organize it

ACTIVITIES

Describing objects, animals and people: When describing objects, animals, or people, we can include any or all the following: number, size, shape, color and location if they're important. For example, if we want to describe the clown on page 2, we could say that it's a clown with a round pink nose and messy brown hair. It has a purple triangle hat with a pink ball on the top. He has two black circle eyes with white dots in the middle. There are two big ears on the side of his head and a smiling mouth with three pink balls in the middle and at each end. That's a complicated description we wouldn't expect from young children but it gives an idea of how features can be described.

Not all the features will be used every time we describe something. Also, as children's language skills develop, they add more features. The table on the next page gives some ideas of what to expect as children mature.

It's often helpful to show your child the kinds of information he should include. Below, you'll find an example (you can get copies on the Self-regulation Everyday website).

Number	Size	Shape	Color	Location
1, 2, 3				

Introduce the idea: "Here's a list of important things when we talk about things." Point to each item on the list and describe one at a time: "Sometimes, we need to

> **Language of spark***
> ....
> Understanding meaning and purpose is encouraged by asking, "Why do you think it's a good idea to include all those things?"
>
> Help your child feel competent with statements like, "Good thinking!", "How did you remember that part?", "You're so clever."

tell how many things, the size, the shape, the color and where it is.

Take turns playing *I Spy, Twenty Questions,* or *Guess Who?* (check the Resources on the website for rules and sources for these and other games).

Typical Age Range++	Parts typically included when describing objects, animals, and people
2 to 3 years	Name of the object, animal or person plus one key feature (number, size, shape, color or location). Example: two dogs (number +object), red ball (color + object), mommy's at work (person + location).
3 to 4 years	Name of the object, animal or person plus two to three key features (number, size, shape, color or location). Example: two brown dogs (number + color + object), big red ball (size + color + object), daddy's black hat is on his head (object + color + location).
4 to 5 years	Name of the object, animal or person plus three to four key features (number, size, shape, color or location). Example: two big brown dogs (number + size + color + object), little red ball on the roof (size + color + object + location).
5 to 6 years	Name of the object, animal or person plus four to five key features (number, size, shape, color or location). Example: two little brown and black sausage dogs (number + size + color + color + shape + object), one big red ball in the store (number + size + color + object + location).
6 to 8 years	Name of the object, animal or person plus more than five key features (number, size, shape, color or location). Example: two big black and white spotted dogs outside (number + size + color + color + color + object + location), one small black and white soccer ball in the middle of the field (number + size + color + color + object + location + location).
++ some children will develop these skills earlier and some later – the age range in this chart is an average. Always start where your child is successful.	

Example → "Let's play *I Spy.* I'll give it a try first and you see if you can tell what I see." Start by including one or two features and see if your child can identify the object in the room. Ask your child to take a turn. Start with one or two key features and prompt him to include as many important ones as possible. Try to keep him from just going through the list and describing all of the features listed if they're not important.

Stories or events: When your child is describing things using at least two features, you can introduce telling stories. It's usually easiest to start with retelling a familiar story from a book or about a recent event in your lives. As children's language skills develop, they add more features to their stories as well as more structure. The table on the next page gives some ideas about how story-telling develops in children and what kinds of things to expect[28].

It's helpful to show your child the information he should include in his story and in what order they need to be included. Below is an example (you'll find a copy on the Self-regulation Everyday website (www.self-reg-everyday.com).

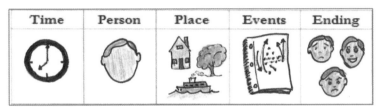

Start by asking your child to retell a story he knows well. Use the storybook to help retell the events. You can also ask him to tell about accidents (for example, how they fell and cut open their head) and incidents (for example, how someone spilled a whole carton of milk on the floor) that have happened to him. You and your child can make your own storybook about these things.

Show him only those pictures appropriate for his age (check the chart on the next page) – cover up the others. If he struggles, cut back on the number of features and try again.

If it seems easy for your child, add more features on your next turn. Be sure to follow the typical development presented in the table on the next page. For young children, only person and place should be expected in

Typical Age Range++	Story parts typically included
2 to 3 years	Lots of ideas that don't always connect to each other. Stories include a main character and a place where the story happens more often. There's no real plot. Example: "The girl lives in this house with her mom and dad. They got two dogs." Use **Person** and **Place** pictures.
3 to 4 years	There's a main character, a place where the story happens and some connection between events. Personal stories often revolve around accidents and incidents. Example: "I was playing outside with my dog and my cat. My cat came up and meowed at me. I cried. Mom came out and said, "Are you okay? What happened?" I told her the cat bited me." Use **Person, Place**, and **Events** pictures.
4 to 5 years	More focus on a sequence of events, usually no high point or climax. Example: "This lady went for a walk. She saw some shoes. The lady said, "Don't clomp at me." Then she seed some pants, a shirt, and some shoes. She said, "I'm not scared." And then she went back home." Use **Person, Place**, and **Events** pictures.
5 to 6 years	Usually a main character and a logical sequence of events. Often no clear ending. Example: "Once upon a time there was a girl named Goldilocks. And she had a grandma who lived in the woods. And Goldilocks' mom told her, "Take this food to grandma". A big bad wolf climbed in grandma's bed. Goldilocks told the wolf that it had big teeth and the wolf tried to eat her. A man came and saved her." Use **Time, Person, Place, Events**, and **Ending** pictures.
6 to 8 years	More stories about real events. True plot and more logical sequence of events. Main characters are described as well as when and where the story takes place. Most stories include a problem that is fixed by the end. Use **Time, Person, Place, Events**, and **Ending** pictures.
++ some children will develop these skills earlier and some later – the age range shown in this chart is an average. Always start where your child is successful.	

the beginning (as shown in the second (Person) and third (Place) pictures in the example above). Once he does that easily, go on to add Events, starting with one or two and adding more each time. Then add Time. Using "Once upon a time", "One time" or "One day" is an easy way to start including an indication of time. When your child can add all those important features with little help from you, add the Ending. Ask him, "How

ILLUSTRATION – seven year old boy (Jack) – continued

Jack is seven so we'd expect well-formed descriptions and stories. He doesn't really like having other people structure him, though. How do you get him to cooperate?

Jack'd probably like barrier games. In playing barrier games, Mom and Jack will sit at opposite sides of a table. They'll have a barrier between them – it could be a book or anything that keeps each of them from seeing what the other person is doing. Each person has the same material on their side of the barrier. With seven-year-old Jack, Mom should expect him to describe five or more main features at a time. A coloring page involving action or athletic heroes would likely work well with him (there are resources on the Self-regulation Everyday website for more barrier games). Jack would tell his mom how to color each item on the page. Jack colors the items at the same time. When describing items, he has to tell what the object is and its number, size, shape, color and location if there are similar objects. Mom should follow just Jack's words and not what she thinks he means. Then they can compare their pictures to see if they're identical. Barrier games give an excellent opportunity for Jack to see how much more clear his messages need to be. He'll likely blame Mom for not listening well so it might be wise to have him give one instruction and then check their pictures rather than waiting until the pictures are finished.

In helping him tell well-structured stories, he'd probably enjoy telling about his athletic exploits or making up a scare story. His mom makes sure she has the strip of pictures showing the important parts to stories. She points to each one if he misses it. Mom could draw a picture of her understanding of Jack's story so she can compare it to what he had in mind. Mom has to be really careful not to fill in missing pieces of information. She needs to draw only what she hears. Mom can also help Jack prepare to tell an important event on the telephone to grandparents. She uses the same Time, Person, Place, Events, and Ending pictures and rehearses the story with him before calling his grandparents. Mom can emphasize that sometimes his grandparents can't understand or see everything so Jack has to be especially clear with them.

ILLUSTRATION – four year old girl (Emma) – continued

Emma likes games like *I Spy* so it's pretty easy to engage her in describing things. She'd also enjoy barrier games. In playing barrier games, Mom and Emma will sit at opposite sides of a table. They'll have a barrier between them – it could be a book or anything that keeps each of them from seeing what the other person is doing. Each person has the same material on their side of the barrier. With four-year-old Emma, it'd be best to start with a simple coloring page. Emma would tell her mom how to color each item on the page. Emma colors the items at the same time. When doing that, she has to describe what the object is and its size, shape and location if there are similar objects. Mom should follow just Emma's words and not what she thinks Emma means. Then they can compare their pictures to see if they're identical. Barrier games give an excellent opportunity for Emma to see how much more clear her messages need to be.

Emma's four so she should be able to tell stories that include person + place + events. She loves to tell stories to her pets and stuffed toys so that might be a good way to start.

Mom shows Emma the list of features that need to be in a story – she covers up the time and ending squares for right now). She explains that her animals will understand better if she tells who's in the story first, then where it takes place and then one or two really important things that happen. Mom lets her know that 'big kids' do this and they add some other things … but not until they can do these three things really well.

Emma has a great imagination so her stories often include things that didn't happen in the story she's referring to or in life. Mom wisely doesn't stop her. She lets her make up stories, just reminding her at the end that it's pretend and what really happened. Imagination is a great thing that shouldn't be stifled. Emma does, however, need help in separating reality and imagined things.

does every story end? You bet, we say, 'and they lived happily ever after'. We have to tell how they feel."

Stage 2 – I can do it here and here

Move on to this stage when your child shows that he can describe objects and tell stories in ways that you'd expect for someone his age.

The goal of this stage is to help your child use his new understanding of how descriptions and stories go together in everyday life. The main executive functions focused on at this stage are:

- inhibitory control – adding more information and not just saying the same old thing

- planning and organization - thinking ahead and planning ahead and organizing the information he wants to tell

- working memory – keeping all the ideas in mind and the features that need to be included as well as the sequence of events

- self-monitoring – checking to make sure all important features are included

ACTIVITIES

Encourage your child to describe things and retell stories and events to other people. Play games, like *I Spy*, *Twenty Questions*, or *Guess Who?*, with other family members and friends. Have your child describe things that happened to him. He can do this in person, via the internet, or on the phone. All these pose different challenges.

Example (skyping with grandma) Make sure you rehearse beforehand so your child doesn't struggle too much. "Why don't' you tell Grandma about your exciting trip to the zoo? She'll really like to hear what happened?" Have the Time-Person-Place-Events-Ending pictures in front of him and get him to go systematically through

> ### Language of spark*
>
> Prompt your child to think on his own with comments like, "You really remembered what to say. What did you tell your brain?"
>
> Help your child feel competent and remind him of the purpose with statements like, "Good thinking!", "You really know how to talk so other people understand."

them when telling his story. Cover up any parts that he hasn't practice yet – for example, if he's two to three years, he'll tell Grandma where he was and a few things he saw but, if he's six to eight, he'll be able to tell all main parts of a well-structured story.

Stage 3 – I can do it even when ...

Move on to this stage after your child shows that his descriptions and storytelling are where they should be for his age.

The goal of this stage is to help your child cope in situations that might challenge the skills he's worked on. The main executive functions focused on at this stage are:

- inhibitory control – talking about the information in order, adding more information and not just saying the same thing

- planning and organization - thinking ahead, planning and organizing the information he wants to talk about

- working memory – keeping all the ideas in mind and the features that need to be included as well as the sequence of events

- self-monitoring – checking to make sure all important features are included

- cognitive flexibility – changing his approach based on the situation

Language of spark*

Help your child become aware of his own thinking by using statements like, "It looks like you're having a hard time remembering all the important things."

Prompt your child to think on his own with comments like, "What could you do to help yourself?"

ACTIVITIES

There are a few ways to increase the challenge. Have him describe an object or tell a story with other people contributing to the description. This can be done in a circle with other people, having each person add the next part of the story. For example, the first person tells the time of the story, the next person tells the main characters, the next adds the setting for the story and so on. Be sure to expect the type and amount of information appropriate to your child's age level (check the chart on page 108 to be sure).

For children from five years of age[29], use the features shown on page 107 to make up riddles. For example, what has hands but can't clap (a watch) or what has one eye but can't see (a needle).

Stage 4 – I can help myself by ...

Move on to this stage when your child shows he can describe things and tell stories in ways you would expect for his age.

The goal of this stage is to help your child support his own skills in different settings by advocating for himself. The main executive functions focused on at this stage are:

- inhibitory control – including all necessary and appropriate information and not just saying the same old thing

- planning and organization - thinking ahead and planning and organizing the information he wants to tell

- working memory – keeping all the ideas in mind and the features that need to be included as well as the sequence of events

- self-monitoring – checking to make sure all important features are included

- cognitive flexibility – changing his approach based on the situation

ACTIVITIES

Now that your child has practiced in different ways with your support, it's time for him to take over more control.

Be ready to prompt him to think of ways to help himself if he's having a difficult time remembering and including important features to his descriptions and stories. For example, he can ask for the strip of pictures that shows the most important pieces of information for descriptions or for stories.

To help children six years and up get away from using the pictures, prompt them to make the pictures in their head. Another strategy is to have them designate one finger on his hand for each feature he has to remember. See the example 'story hand' below.

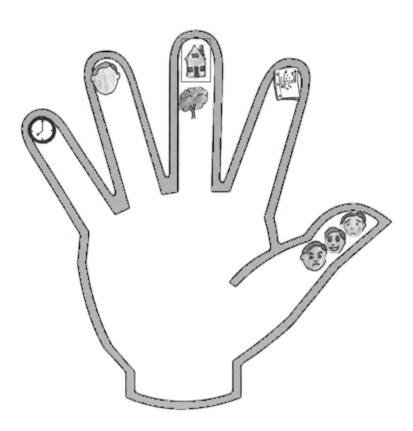

6 Emotional Self-Regulation

Your child now has a solid base of body self-regulation and cognitive self-regulation. He knows how to calm his body and brain, focus his attention, and make sure he understands what's going on. We're ready to move into the realm of emotions.

Facial expressions communicate a great deal about our emotional state. If you don't understand what these mean, making your way through the social world is much more difficult. The ability to recognize facial expressions and emotions is crucial to establishing connections with other people. It's one of the main ways to understand the feelings and intentions of other people. Understanding how we feel and how someone else is feeling gives us valuable information about how to adapt our behavior.

The ability to recognize your own and other people's emotions, understand what may have caused the feelings, and respond appropriately to your own and the other person's emotions, is referred to as Emotional Intelligence (EI)[30]. It's a useful framework for developing emotional self-regulation. We'll tackle four basic stages[31] in the development of emotional self-regulation:

1. **Self-awareness:** Self-awareness and self-knowledge are important features of emotional self-regulation. You need to notice and recognize your own emotions and name them. Interestingly, children

115

who can recognize and label emotions as preschoolers are found to be better adjusted and better behaved four years later[32]. This suggests that just learning about and recognizing your own emotions can have an important impact on social skills.

2. **Empathy:** This is the ability to recognize emotions in other people and put yourself in their 'emotional shoes'. Empathy plays an important role in social understanding[33,34] and is a foundation for positive relationships[35]. It's also an important part in achievement in school[36,37]. Empathy motivates helping, sharing, cooperation and other behavior that benefits other people[38] ('pro-social behavior').

3. **Meaning:** This is the ability to understand the meaning and cause of different emotions. Not only do children have to identify emotions through facial expressions, they need to understand what may have caused them - why person is happy, sad, angry, or frightened. It's critical to have some understanding of possible causes in order to respond appropriately. For example, a person may look angry and you need to figure out whether the anger is directed at you, himself, or some event in his life. By doing that, you can find an appropriate way to respond.

4. **Managing:** Children need to learn to control and express their emotions in ways that are appropriate to the situation. We don't want children to stifle how they feel but, instead, learn how and when to express their feelings. They also need to learn how to respond to other people's emotions in appropriate ways. These involve exploring strategies for responding so that relationships with others are as harmonious as possible. For example, if someone looks sad, your child may ask what happened, may hug the other person and ask if he's okay, or simply say, "I'm sorry".

In the Emotional Self-Regulation unit, we want your child to learn to make good social and emotional decisions.

In order to do that, we'll help him develop skills and knowledge in all four of the areas above.

In the information that follows, you'll find out more about each goal and where and when you might practice the skills with your child. There are activities you can do with him to improve his emotional self-regulation and resources that you can use for practicing.

> Be sure to continue Turtle Breathing in everyday situations, during yoga and while practicing these new skills.

Order of skills

1. First, self-awareness (knowing our feelings and recognizing emotions when they arise).

2. Next, empathy (recognizing others' emotions and being able to put yourself in someone else's 'emotional shoes')

3. Then, meaning (interpreting meanings and causes of emotions)

4. Finally, managing (controlling and expressing emotions appropriately and responding to other people's emotions in appropriate ways).

In all activities, the main goal is for your child to develop and use emotional self-regulation strategies. For this reason, we'll use a small set of basic emotions that are universal to most cultures and nationalities[39]. They include the following six key emotions:

- happiness,
- sadness,
- anger,
- fear,
- surprise, and
- disgust.

Stage 1 – I can do it!

The goal of these activities is to help your child learn to recognize his own emotions and name them accurately. We'll also help him use facial expressions to let other people know how he feels. He's already worked on focusing his attention and looking for signals, clues, and models so facial expressions are a natural next step – facial expressions are social signals..

The main executive functions included in these activities are:

- inhibitory control – stopping himself in order to focus on his facial expressions

- working memory – taking in information about his facial expression and 'match' it with an appropriate name/label

- self-monitoring – recognizing his different feelings

Language of spark*

....

Prompt him to demonstrate his thinking and his understanding of the main features of each emotion by saying, "Why do you think I look happy?" This will also give you information about how he's thinking and what kind of clarification might be needed.

Children begin naming emotions before their second birthday[40]. Two-year olds can tell the difference between and discuss a variety of emotions[41]. They use some emotion names accurately[42] and talk about their own and others' feelings[43]. They can also give emotions to dolls, toy animals[44] and their siblings during pretend play[45]. This doesn't mean, however, that their understanding is adult-like. Young children may say they're angry but mean something that's negative but not angry the way adults would interpret it. They may say they're angry when they're surprised by something or say they're surprised when they're happy. They're likely to confuse positive emotions with other positive emotions (happiness and surprise) and negative with negative (anger, fear, and sadness)[46]. It's not until children are about 10 that they're skilled in identifying different emotions from facial expressions[47].

Ages at which children develop a solid understanding of different emotions is presented in the next table. These are the age ranges when children show a solid understanding of the features and qualities of each feeling**[48]**. They may have used names for some of the emotions before each age range but likely didn't fully understand their true meanings. Use this table to figure out which emotions you and your child will focus on. For example, if he's 4 ½, introduce happy, sad, angry, and scared but not surprised or disgusted.

Typical Age Range++	Recognize and Name Key Emotions
2 to 3 years	Happy, sad, angry
3 to 4 years	Happy, sad, angry
4 to 5 years	Happy, sad, angry, scared
5 to 6 years	Happy, sad, angry, scared, surprised
6 to 8 years	Happy, sad, angry, scared, surprised, disgusted
++ some children will develop these skills earlier and some later – the age range is an average that's only meant to guide you.	

ACTIVITIES

Tell your child, "We're going to see how you're feeling. We'll look at your face and see if we can tell how you feel. Let's give it a try."

Use a mirror to help him see his facial expressions. Ask him to show you each of the expressions you're working on. Point out how you can recognize each emotion, using the chart of main features on the next page. We keep the features to three basic ones so he has clear, simple guidelines.

Example ➤ "We're going to look at our faces to see how we're feeling. I think you look happy. I can see your eyebrows are up a little bit, your eyes are open and your mouth is turning up. Let's look in the mirror". Look in the mirror with your child, checking his eyebrows, eyes and mouth. Then check your own happy face, again pointing out your eyebrows, eyes and mouth. Ask your child to show you one of the other expressions you're focusing on. Comment on his eyebrows, eyes and mouth and how they help tell how he's feeling. Do this with each facial expression that's appropriate for his age group. If he has problems making any of the expressions, show him how you do it and ask him to imitate.

Emotion	Main features		
	eyebrows	eyes	mouth
happy	raised	open slightly	corners up
sad	lowered	slightly closed	corners turned down slightly
afraid	raised	open wide	open
angry	lowered	slightly closed	corners turned down
surprise	raised	open wide	open
disgust	lowered a little, wrinkles between	slightly closed	corners turned down (nose may also be wrinkled)

Have him name each emotion as you and he make the different facial expressions. Make this into a 'guess-this-emotion' game where he makes a different facial expression and you have to guess which emotion it is. Take turns and be sure to make it fun and engaging.

Use storybooks, magazines and videos to find people looking happy, sad, angry, etc. Talk about how you know what these people and characters are feeling, using the main features in the chart above.

If he names an emotion other than what you expect, say, "Hmm, that's interesting. Why do you think you look (emotion)?" This way you can figure out what features are causing him some confusion. The two of you can then look for different examples of the facial expressions from magazines and books and sort them into categories. This will help him understand the differences and similarities among the facial expressions.

Stage 2 – I can do it here and here

Move on to this stage when your child shows he reliably identifies and names the key emotions for his age group.

The goal of this stage is to help your child recognize others' emotions and put himself in their 'emotional shoes'. This is the beginning of empathy.

True empathy takes time to develop. Young children will become upset if they see another person in distress. At this stage, children usually can't tell the difference between someone else's experience and their own. When someone cries, he may cry also. This isn't true empathy.

After about two years of age, children start to separate other people's experiences from their own. It's around this time that they'll try to comfort someone who's upset. Between three to eight years of age, children become more aware of other people's feelings and how their perspective may be different from their own[49] (that is, something may upset the other person that doesn't even bother you). A truer form of empathy is emerging. Children even start feeling empathy for people and animals in books, in movies, and on television.

These changes in developing empathy mean that, for two to three year olds, you'll expect an emotion that is a direct expression of their own experiences. After three years of age, there's a slow increase in understanding that other people may experience different emotions. Keep most examples and experiences you discuss related to real events and those shown in books or movies. With children over five years, you can start

Language of spark*

Ensure your child has a feeling of competence by saying things like, "That's a really good idea. I hadn't thought of that."

By choosing and taking different roles in reenacting storybooks and videos, your child will feel like he's sharing participation in the activity.

Make sure your child is thinking on his own and demonstrating his knowledge by asking him to explain how he knows that someone is feeling a certain way ("How do you know he's sad?").

introducing hypothetical situations (for example, "What if this boy ran away? How would his mom feel?").

The main executive functions practiced at this stage are:

• inhibitory control - making sure he listens and looks carefully and doesn't get distracted by other things

• working memory – taking in information about the person or character's facial expression and connecting his own experiences and feelings with those of the person or character

• self-monitoring - checking to make sure he's taking in all important pieces of information and putting them together

• cognitive flexibility - changing to take on the feelings of another person or character

ACTIVITIES

The main focus in these activities will be role-playing. This will let your child take someone else's position and experience their emotions.

Storybooks and videos are excellent media to use for learning and talking about empathy. They're enjoyable, repeatable and the characters aren't real. It makes emotions, especially negative emotions, easier to witness when they're not 'real'. Start with books and videos that include experiences your child has had. For example, he felt sad when he fell and skinned his knee, happy when he got his new bike, angry when someone took his toy. It's easier for him to relate to things he's actually experienced.

Suggested books are included on the Self-regulation Everyday website (www.self-reg-everyday.com). You can also find books that cover the topics you want by going to the Children's Picture Book Database at http://dlp.lib.miamioh.edu/picturebook/. The database includes books for preschoolers through to age eight. You can search by emotions or experiences (like 'new bike') and find lists of possible books to choose from.

Read the book or watch the video a few times so your child is familiar with the story. Then each of you choose a role to act out. Make sure you exaggerate the emotions and make it fun – be drama queens! Discuss how the person feels and how their face shows that emotion.

When you're at home or out in the community with your child, comment about how people around you seem to be feeling. Ask him how he thinks different people are feeling.

Stage 3 – I can do it even when ...

Move on to this stage after your child shows that he can consistently identify and name the key emotions that other people and characters experience.

The goal of this stage is to help your child interpret meanings and causes of emotions. He needs to figure out the possible reasons for different feelings before we go on to learning how to respond to them.

There are some fairly universal reasons why we experience different emotions. If we receive something we really want, that generally makes us feel happy. You can feel happy if you avoid something negative, like getting a better grade on a test than you thought you would. The main reasons for each of the target emotions are presented in the table on the next page. Be sure to check back to page 121 to remind yourself of appropriate expectations for different age groups.

The main executive functions focused on at this stage are:

- inhibitory control - making sure he listens and looks carefully and isn't distracted by less important information

Language of spark*

Understanding meaning and purpose and thinking on his own is encouraged by asking, "Why do you think that person is feeling (emotion)?"

Help your child feel competent with statements like, "Good thinking!", "How did you know that?", "You're so clever."

Remember to avoid using the words 'no', 'not' and 'don't' during the activities. These words tend to stop children from thinking on their own.

- working memory – connecting experiences and events to his emotions and those of others
- cognitive flexibility – finding reasons for emotions that may not be in his own experience

Feeling/Emotion	Typical reason for feeling/emotion
Happy	<ul><li>Get something you want</li><li>Avoid something unpleasant</li></ul>
Sad	<ul><li>Lose something or someone you like</li></ul>
Angry	<ul><li>Don't get something you value or want</li><li>When someone intentionally hurts you</li></ul>
Scared	<ul><li>Something threatens your safety</li></ul>
Surprised	<ul><li>Something happens that you didn't expect (can be positive or negative)</li></ul>
Disgusted	<ul><li>You come across something unpleasant</li></ul>

ACTIVITIES

The main focus in these activities will be identifying reasons for emotions in your child and other people and characters. This will help him start connecting the emotions to events causing them, deepening his sense of empathy.

Storybooks or videos are excellent media to use for learning and talking about reasons for each emotion. They let your child have some 'emotional distance' from the events – we don't want him to become upset during these activities. Since the characters aren't real, your child can look at the dilemmas as humorous or, at least, not distressing.

Find books or videos that include the emotions you're practicing with your child. Suggested books are included on the Self-regulation Everyday website (www.self-reg-everyday.com). You can also find books that cover the topics you want by going to the Children's Picture Book Database at http://dlp.lib.miamioh.edu/picturebook/. Search the database with terms that include the emotion plus situation (for example, happy + bike, scared/afraid + ghost).

Read a book or view a video a few times so that your child's familiar with the story. Then, as you review it, ask him how a character feels. Next ask him why he thinks that ("Why do you think he feels that way?", "What made him feel that way?"). Be sure to use the reasons given in the table on the previous page at least to start with. Once your child learns the basics, you can move on to more refined or specific reasons.

Example (something happens to a family member) Comment, "Wow, look what happened to him. How do you think he feels?" Praise your child if he identifies the emotion correctly. If he's not sure how the person feels, remind him about how the person's eyebrows, eyes and mouth looked and what happened to him. Help him put these clues together to come up with a likely feeling. Next ask him, "Why do you think he feels that way? What happened?" If he gives you a reasonable answer, praise him for good thinking and share your thoughts about the reasons. If he's not sure why they might be feeling a certain way, help him think about the situation and what happened: "Well, let's think. You said he was surprised. Now, why do you think he felt surprised?" If he continues to have problems figuring out the reason, related the emotion to him, asking, "What happens to surprise you?" and try to highlight important parts of the incident that might be familiar to your child.

Stage 4 – I can help myself by ...

Move on to this stage when your child shows he has a fairly solid grasp of what may cause the key emotions you're focusing on.

The goal of this stage is to help your child respond appropriately to his own and other's emotions. This means working directly on emotional self-regulation. You've helped your child identify and name emotions, feel how other people might experience different emotions, and understand why people feel each of the key emotions. Now we'll put all of this together and figure out how to respond in ways that are appropriate.

The main executive functions focused on at this stage are:

- inhibitory control - making sure he listens and looks carefully so he understands the situation and possible causes of the emotion and controls his emotional reaction so he can respond appropriately

- planning and organization - thinking about ways he can respond to his own emotions and those of other people

- working memory – connecting experiences and events to emotions expressed by your child and by other people and recalling how he might respond

- self-monitoring - checking to see how he's doing, especially in relation to his own emotional self-regulation

- cognitive flexibility – responding to situations that may not be in his own experience, changing and adapting to different situations and people

---

Language of spark*

....

Prompt your child to think on his own with comments like, "If you fell and hurt your knee, what should I do?" Model statements like, "I know that really hurts and I don't want you to feel sad. I think I'll take a Turtle Breath and stay calm and then ask you if I can get a bandage."

Help your child feel competent with statements like, "Good thinking!", "You really know how to figure out how she feels and what you can do. I think you helped her feel better."

Give your child lots of chances to demonstrate what he knows. Try your best to stand back, helping him out only when necessary.

ACTIVITIES

Now that your child has learned self-awareness, empathy and meaning of different key emotions, we move on to helping him learn how to manage his own emotions and respond to others.

For emotions in others: Explain to him, "You know how to tell what different feelings are and what might make them happen. You also know how to make your body and your brain be calm and figure out what to do. We're going to see how we can help other people if they're feeling sad or angry or happy."

Use storybooks and videos to practice. First, have him identify the emotions of a character, then the reason for it and, finally, explore ways you and your child might respond to the person. For example, if the person won something and feels happy, you could help your child congratulate them. If they fell and hurt their knee, you could suggest your child ask if he can help. If they're feeling sad, you could prompt your child to say he's sorry they're feeling sad and ask if there's any way he can help. Select ways of responding that are appropriate for your child's age and to your culture and your family. The most important thing is that your child responds with some understanding and empathy.

For emotions in himself: There are a number of different ways to help your child deal with his own emotions. There are times when he should get an adult to help him and times when he should help himself. Times when he should get help from an adult likely include if he gets hurt or has an accident or if someone bothers, teases, or bullies him. Decide on these things with your child, making a list of times when he should get help from an adult.

In all situations, he needs to stay as calm as possible so he can make better decisions about what to do. Turtle Breathing is the most practiced and simplest technique for your child to use. He's been using it since the

ILLUSTRATION – seven year old boy (Jack) – continued

Jack is a fellow who needs lots of help in this department. He likes to make negative comments about things which often aren't appreciated by other people. It seems that sometimes the comments are based in his insecurities and sometimes he just seems to like arousing reactions in other people. He's prone to saying negative things about things other people have. If someone talks about something new and exciting in their lives, he'll often comment how he already has it or make some other disparaging remark. He'll also call many things 'boring' seemingly to pass them off as unimportant. Jack is also known to start acting up at family gatherings. He'll make silly faces or noises, seemingly to gain attention or to stir other people up. He does this until an adult reprimands him, ignoring doesn't seem to work.

Jack really needs help with emotional self-regulation. Since working on body and cognitive self-regulation, his general control has improved but old habits die hard. The first step should be to review emotions and make sure he can consistently identify them (how does Dad's face look when he's starting to become annoyed with you?). It seems like he doesn't recognize increasing annoyance and anger in other people until there's some explosion of emotion. Next, he needs to understand how someone else feels when he behaves in certain ways or says certain things. A good first step would be to enact storybooks or videos that depict these situations. After that, it needs to be personalized with him – "How would you feel if …" After working on these areas, he needs some strategies. He would benefit from work on putting some thoughts away, like in a Brain Box. Help him understand that using 'mean' words and saying negative things hurt other people's feelings. He'll also need to understand that other people won't want to be around him if he says 'mean' things. He'll need to be reassured, however, that he is a terrific fellow and lots of people love him. He may say that other people are bothering him and making him behave in certain ways. This is where a shield could help.

With Jack, it's important to help him understand the impact of his behavior on other people. Over time, it'll be important to work on the apparent insecurities that give rise to these behaviors.

ILLUSTRATION – four year old girl (Emma) – continued

Emma tends to speak her mind, having little idea how it might impact other people. She needs lots of work on identifying emotions correctly so she can understand better how people are responding to her. Then work should focus on gaining some empathy – how she would feel if someone said that to her. Role-playing with Mom using storybooks and videos will be a good format. Helping her act out and sense how someone else may feel will be an important learning process. Emma will be helped with the rule that sometimes it's better to put things in your Brain Box than say it. That way, people won't feel sad or angry.

beginning of this journey in self-regulation. He can now use it to calm himself so his emotions don't spill over and interfere with his ability to advocate for himself.

There are three main ways of dealing with situations. They include: (1) stopping emotions that aren't helpful and/or appropriate at that moment or in that situation, (2) putting the emotion away until later so he can get help interpreting and understanding them, and (3) explaining how he feels.

1. ***Stopping emotions*. Ignoring** things that aren't important is a skill your child learned earlier in Cognitive self-regulation. It's an effective strategy for helping himself stay calm and not be bothered by things, people, or events around him. Ignoring is a strategy to help stop himself from becoming upset long enough to get some help or to think things through. If other children around him are getting

upset or over-excited, he can ignore them so he can get his work done. Some children can become so swept up in emotions around them that they can't concentrate. They may become upset by events that don't involve them (for example, when a teacher or parent reprimands another child). Parents need to judge for themselves what things their children should ignore. We don't want childrent to block themselves off from emotions but there are times when they don't need to be swept up in them (like when another child is being 'silly'(.

Another strategy to help him ignore things is using a **Shield**. Construct a simple cardboard shield that looks like something used by a superhero or superheroine. Explain to him, "Shields are really strong and things just bounce off them. A shield can help so things don't bug/bother you." Practice

130

bugging him and having him hold up his shield to make the words bounce off. After practicing a few times, he can either make a very small shield that can fit in his pocket or use an 'invisible' (pretend) one for day to day situations. Parents need to judge for themselves what things their children should use the shield for.

2. ***Putting emotions away until later***. There are some situations when your child might feel a certain way but it isn't the right time for a meltdown, gales of laughter or buckets of tears. We don't want him to stifle his feelings, just delay them.

   One helpful strategy is a **Brain Box.** That is a special box where he can put his emotions and/or the things that are causing them. Explain to him, "Sometimes, things bug or bother us and it makes it hard to think. We can just take them out of our brains and put them in your Brain Box. It's safe in the box and we can take it out again if we want to." He can put happy thoughts or sad, angry, scared thoughts in the Brain Box. This will give him a chance to move on with what he needs to do and deal with the problem later. Sometimes, children will be distracted by exciting events that are coming up so the Brain Box can help him put those away for a little while. The main idea of the Brain Box is to keep feelings from interfering with what he's doing at this moment but also not deny the feelings. He can just put them away temporarily until he can talk with an adult or advocate for himself calmly.

   The second strategy is **Happy Thoughts bubbles**. A Happy Thought bubble is a way to help your child restore himself. Explain to your child that, if he feels sad, scared, or angry, he can help himself feel better at important times by thinking only about things that make him happy. Make a thought bubble with your child (make it small enough to fit in his pocket so he can take it anywhere) and help him draw or put pictures of his favorite objects, people, and/or

activities that make him feel happy. Some children choose a picture of their dog; others choose a favorite cartoon character. It's up to each child. Have him put a few drawings or pictures on his thought bubble. You can make your own at the same time. Practice filling your brain bubbles with the things that make you feel happy while using your Turtle Breathing. After using it a few times, your child may be able to picture his Thought Bubble in his brain without taking his bubble with him.

3. ***Explaining how and why he feels a certain way.*** As children mature and their language skills develop, they can begin explaining how they feel and why. These are excellent opportunities for you to discuss these feelings and how he might help himself deal with them in appropriate ways. These may be feelings he collected on his Thought Bubble or in his Brain Box. To help your child develop his emotional self-regulation, he'll need your help in understanding what may have caused feelings he or other people experience and how to respond appropriately. Make sure your child feels comfortable discussing emotions with you because you can provide important guidance to him. Your child can also use his ability to explain his feelings to help other people understand how they're impacting him. He can ask other people to stop doing something because it makes him feel angry or afraid. Being able to explain the impact of other people's behavior and/or events, he can advocate for himself. You'll need to help him determine when and where he should do this as it could backfire in some situations (with a bully).

7 Continuing the journey

We started this journey with a goal to help you and your child develop his self-regulation in everyday situations.

We found that self-regulation is more than just stopping or controlling your child's actions, thoughts and emotions. It's not just learned self-control or a form of behavior management. Self-regulation is also more than just keeping himself alert and aware of himself.

Self-regulation involves the executive functions; those parts of the brain's frontal lobes that let us translate thoughts and ideas into actions. Learning self-regulation includes learning how to deliberately:

- control impulses,
- plan and organize your thoughts and actions,
- remember what you're doing and put your ideas together,
- check how you're doing while you work
- be flexible enough to change directions if needed

Children are born curious and striving for independence. If we help guide them, they can learn to regulate their own attention, thoughts, actions, and emotions.

Self-regulation doesn't just happen. It takes time and practice. Every time our children take on new challenges, they have to adjust their self-regulation according to those settings and demands. It's something most people work on throughout their lives, changing as their life circumstances change.

In *Self-regulation in Everyday Life*, we've focused on self-regulation rather than teaching children specific learning strategies. This means we shifted from teaching specific behaviors to working on foundation skills. We've found in our research that, by focusing on executive functions, self-regulation spreads to all areas of functioning. For example, when we worked with children on body self-regulation, there were significant changes in their social and cognitive skills in addition to improvements in behavior. We believe that working through the four stages of self-awareness ("I can do it"), understanding when and where he needs to use his new skills ("I can do it here and here."), practicing in more challenging places ("I can do it even when ..."), and advocating for himself ("I can help myself by ...") builds more enduring learning.

By helping children learn to "maintain their motivation and keep themselves on-task in the face of competing demands and attractions (they) should learn better than students who are less skilled at regulating"[50]. Self-regulated learners show some unique capabilities[51,52,53,54,55,56,57], including:

1. Knowing how and when to use different cognitive strategies to help themselves take in information completely, organize it, elaborate it, and use it.

2. Knowing how to plan, control and direct themselves so they achieve their goals.

3. Having a sense of self-efficacy (belief in their own abilities) and positive feelings toward learning.

4. Planning and controlling their time and effort, knowing how to create and structure learning situations to make it easier to think and work, such as locating a quiet place to read or asking for help from a teacher.

5. Using strategies that reduce distractions so they can maintain their concentration, effort, and motivation while working.

Self-regulated children tend to be self-starters who are confident, strategic and resourceful. One study[58] that followed a group of more than 1,000 children over 30 years found that those who had stronger self-regulation as youngsters were healthier, wealthier, and more socially responsible as adults. That's a strong endorsement for helping your child improve his self-regulation.

A few things to remember

Continue using the Language of spark*. This is the number one thing to remember. Using these words and ways of talking make a larger difference than you may realize. If you're consistent, you'll see differences in understanding and cooperation in your child. As often as possible, ask your child questions rather than tell him what to do. For example, instead of telling him to take his coat and hang it up, ask him. "What do you need to do with your coat?" It makes sure he's thinking and increases the chances that you won't have to remind him next time. To help you, we've put some Language of spark* cue cards in the Resources files on the Self-regulation Everyday website.

Be sure to make Turtle Breathing and yoga part of your child's everyday life. He should use it before starting something challenging, if he's becoming upset, and at other times when he needs to be calm and centered (such as bedtime). Any time his body, thinking, and emotions might become dysregulated is a good time to do some Turtle Breathing. Slow, calm breathing is something he can use throughout his life.

Remember you need to catch your child before he becomes too dysregulated, upset, excited, busy, or scattered to remind him to self-regulate.

Self-regulation is hard work for children and they need proper fuel so make sure he's nourished and rested. If he's hungry and/or tired, don't expect him to self-regulate for long.

Keep practicing fun. Activities should last no longer than the number of minutes equal to twice his age (that is, if he's four, the activity shouldn't last more than eight minutes). Be sure to include things he likes in practice activities. Your child will also be more motivated if you make sure he understands the reason and purpose for things you do with him, make sure he feels competent, and has a sense of control.

Think out loud. Help your child understand that you use self-regulation too. Let him hear what you think when you're keeping yourself on track or completing something. Make sure he hears about times when you forget to self-regulate. For example, "Darn, I wasn't systematic so I missed that part."

Give your child some responsibilities around your household. He's a member of the family and all members need to keep things going at home. As you saw on the lists on pages 72-73, there are many different things he can do to help out, regardless of age. Having household tasks can help develop his self-regulation, life skills (a future partner will thank you), his sense of independence, and his social responsibility.

Stand back and let your child try things on his own. If he makes a mistake, it's just another chance for learning. Errors should be treated as 'oops' moments rather than tragedies. They're times when he needs to think again about how he should approach the task. Mistakes are important parts of learning.

Teach him to be more resilient and cope in different situations. That's what we focused on during the "I can do it even when ..." stages. He learned that, even in situations that aren't ideal, he can continue on. He also can advocate for himself to make things easier, just like we worked on during the "I can help myself by ..." stage.

All of these things mean that you have to continue working on your own self-regulation. Remind yourself of the things listed on page 34.

Now that you've worked with your child on his self-regulation, do the *Executive Function Survey* (pages 7 and 8) again and see what changes your child has made

Index

References

1 MacKenzie, H. (2013). *The Autistic Child's Guide: Presenting spark* (Self-regulation Program of Awareness & Resilience in Kids)*. St. Catharines, Ontario: Wired Fox Publications.

2 Tangney, J. P., Baumeister, R. F., & Boone, A. L. (2004). High self-control predicts good adjustment, less pathology, better grades, and interpersonal success. *Journal of Personality, 72,* 271–324.

3 Levesque, C. S., Zuehlke, N., Stanek, L., & Ryan, R. M. (2004). Autonomy and competence in German and U.S. university students: A comparative study based on self-determination theory. *Journal of Educational Psychology, 96,* 68-84

4 Ryan, R. M., Connell, J. P., & Plant, R. W. (1990). Emotions in non-directed text learning. *Learning and Individual Differences, 2,* 1-17.

5 Baumeister, R. F., DeWall, C. N., Ciarocco, N. J., & Twenge, J. M. (2005). Social exclusion impairs self-regulation. *Journal of Personality and Social Psychology, 88,* 589 – 604.

6 Baumeister, R. F., & Vohs, K. D. (2007). Self-regulation, ego-depletion, and motivation. *Social and Personality Psychology Compass, 1,* 115–128

7 Deci, E. L., Koestner, R., & Ryan, R. M. (1999). A meta-analytic review of experiments examining the effects of extrinsic rewards on intrinsic motivation. *Psychological Bulletin, 125,* 627–668.

8 Reeve, J., Jang, H., Harde, P., & Omura, M. (2002). Providing a rationale in an autonomy-supportive way as a strategy to motivate others during an uninteresting activity. *Motivation and Emotion, 26,* 183-207.

9 Reeve, J., Deci, E. L., & Ryan, R. M. (2004). Self-determination theory: A dialectical framework for understanding socio-cultural influences on student motivation. In S. Van Etten & M. Pressley (Eds.), *Big theories revisited* (pp. 31–60). Greenwich, CT: Information Age Press.

10 Assor, A., Kaplan, H., Roth, G., & Kanat-Maymon, Y. (2005) Directly Controlling Teacher Behaviors as Predictors of Poor Motivation and Engagement in Girls and Boys: The Role of Anger and anxiety. *Learning and Instruction*, 15, 396- 412.

11 Martin, J. E., Mithaug, D. E., Cox, P., Peterson, L. Y., Van Dyke, J. L., & Cash, M. E. (2003). Increasing self-determination: Teaching students to plan, work, evaluate, and adjust. *Exceptional Children*, 69(4), 431–447.

12 Pelletier, L. G., Fortier, M. S., Vallerand, R. J., & Brière, N. M. (2001). Associations among perceived autonomy support, forms of self-regulation, and persistence: A prospective study. *Motivation and Emotion*, 25, 279-306.

13 Patrick, B. C., Skinner, E. A., & Connell, J. P. (1993). What motivates children's behavior and emotion? The joint effects of perceived control and autonomy in the academic domain. Journal of *Personality and Social Psychology*, 65 (4), 781–791.

14 Reeve, J., Jang, H., Harde, P., & Omura, M. (2002). Providing a rationale in an autonomy-supportive way as a strategy to motivate others during an uninteresting activity. *Motivation and Emotion*, 26, 183-207.

15 Ryan, R. M., & Connell, J. P. (1989). Perceived locus of causality and internalization: Examining reasons for acting in two domains. *Journal of Personality and Social Psychology*, 57, 749-761.

16 Hardré, P. L., & Reeve, J. (2003). A motivational model of rural students' intentions to persist in, versus drop out, of high school, *Journal of Educational Psychology*, 95(2), 347-356.

17 Noels, K.A., L.G. Pelletier, R. Clément and R.J. Vallerand. 2000. Why are you learning a second language? Motivational orientations and self-determination theory. *Language Learning*, 50, pp. 57–85

18 Sowers, J., & Powers, L. (1995). Enhancing the participation and independence of students with severe physical and multiple disabilities in performing community activities. *Mental Retardation*, 33, 209–220

19 MacKenzie, H. (2013). *The Autistic Child's Guide: Presenting spark* (Self-regulation Program of Awareness & Resilience in Kids)*. St. Catharines, Ontario: Wired Fox Publications.

20 Check out the research results on **spark*** at http://www.self-reg-everyday.com

21 Bierman, K., Torres, M. & Scholfield, H. (2010). Developmental Factors Related to the Assessment of Social Skills. In D. Nangle, D. Hansen, C. Erdley. & P. Norton (Eds.). *Practitioner's Guide to Empirically Based Measures of Social Skills*. New York: Springer Science+Business Media.

22 Eisenberg, N., & Fabes, R. A. (1992). Emotion, regulation, and the development of social competence. In M. Clark (Ed.), *Review of personality and social psych.: Emotion and social behavior*. Newbury Park, CT: Sage

23 Eisenberg, N., & Fabes, R. A. (1992). Emotion, regulation, and the development of social competence. In M. Clark (Ed.), *Review of personality and social Psych.: Emotion and social behavior*. Newbury Park, CT: Sage

24 Bierman, K., Torres, M. & Scholfield, H. (2010). Developmental Factors Related to the Assessment of Social Skills. In D. Nangle, D. Hansen, C. Erdley. & P. Norton (Eds.). *Practitioner's Guide to Empirically Based Measures of Social Skills*. New York: Springer Science+Business Media.

25 Deci, E. L., Koestelr, R., & Ryan, R. M. (1999). A meta-analytic review of experiments examining the effects of extrinsic rewards on intrinsic motivation. *Psychological Bulletin*, 125, 627-668.

26 Source: http://www.asha.org/public/speech /development/chart.htm

27 Source: http://www.asha.org/uploadedFiles/Build-Your-Childs-Skills-Kindergarten-to-Second-Grade.pdf

28 Schneider, P., Dubé, R., & Hayward, D. (2005). *Edmonton Narrative Norms Instrument.* Edmonton, Alberta: University of Alberta.

29 McGhee, P. E. (1979). *Humor: Its origin and development.* San Francisco: W.H. Freeman & Co.

30 Goleman, D. (1995). *Emotional Intelligence.* New York: Bantam.

31 Mayer, J. D. & Salovey, P. (2007) What is emotional intelligence? In P. Salovey & D. Sluyter (Eds.). *Emotional development and emotional intelligence: Educational implications.* New York: Basic Books.

32 Izard, C., Fine, S., Schultz, D., Mostow, A., Ackerman, B., & Youngstrom, E. (2001). Emotion knowledge as a predictor of social behavior and academic competence in children at risk. *Psychological Science,* 12, p. 18–23.

33 Schonert-Reichl, K. A. (1999). Moral reasoning during early adolescence: Links with peer acceptance, friendship, and social behaviors. *Journal of Early Adolescence,* 19, 249–279.

34 Schultz, L. H., Selman, R. L., & LaRusso, M. D. (2003). The assessment of psychosocial maturity in children and adolescents: Implications for the evaluation of school-based character education programs. *Journal of Research in Character Education,* 1, 67-87.

35 Schonert-Reichl, K. A. (1993). Empathy and social relationships in adolescents with behavioral disorders. *Behavioral Disorders,* 18, 189–204.

36 Caprara, G. V., Barbanelli, C., Pastorelli, C., Bandura, A, & Zimbardo, P. G. (2000). Prosocial foundations of children's academic achievement. *Psychological Science,* 11, 302–306.

37 Wentzel, K. R. (1993). Does being good make the grade? Social behavior and academic competence in middle school. *Journal of Educational Psychology,* 85, 357–364.

38 Eisenberg, N. (1982). The development of reasoning about prosocial behavior. In N. Eisenberg (Ed.), *The development of prosocial behavior* (pp. 219-249). New York: Academic Press

39 Ekman, P., Sorenson, E. R., & Friesen, W. V. (1969). Pan-Cultural Elements In Facial Display Of Emotions. *Science*, 164, 86-88.

40 Ridgeway, D., Waters, E., & Kuczaj II, S. A. (1985). Acquisition of emotion-descriptive language: Receptive and productive vocabulary norms for ages 18 months to 6 years. *Developmental Psychology*, 21, 901-908

41 Dunn, J., Bretherton, I., & Munn, P. (1987). Conversations about feeling states between mothers and their young children. *Developmental Psychology*, 23.

42 Ridgeway, D., Waters, E., & Kuczaj II, S. A. (1985). Acquisition of emotion-descriptive language: Receptive and productive vocabulary norms for ages 18 months to 6 years. *Developmental Psychology*, 21, 901-908.

43 Bretherton, I., Fritz, J., Zahn-Waxler, C., & Ridgeway, D. (1986). Learning to talk about emotions: A functional perspective. *Child Development*, 57, 529-548.

44 Wolf, D. P., Rygh, J., & Altshuler, J. (1984). Agency and experience: Actions and states in play narratives. In I. Bretherton (Ed.), *Symbolic play: The development of social understanding* (pp. 195–217). New York: Academic Press, Inc.

45 Dunn, J., Bretherton, I., & Munn, P. (1987). Conversations about feeling states between mothers and their young children. *Developmental Psychology*, 23, 791-798.

46 Most, T., Bachar, D., & Dromi, E. (2011). Auditory, Visual, and Auditory-Visual Identification of Emotions by Nursery School Children. *Journal of Speech-Language Pathology and Applied Behavior Analysis*, 5(1), 25–34.

47 Thomas, L. A., De Bellis, M. D., Graham, R., and LaBar, K. S. (2007). Development of emotional facial recognition in late childhood and adolescence. *Developmental Science,* 10, 547–558.

48 Widen, S. C., & Russell, J. a. (2008). Children acquire emotion categories gradually. *Cognitive Development,* 23, 291–312.

49 Hoffman, M. L. (1984). Interaction of affect and cognition in empathy. In C. E. Izard, J. Kagan, & R. B. Zajonc (Eds.), *Emotions, cognitions, and behavior* (pp. 103-131). Cambridge: Cambridge University Press.

50 Dornyei, Z. (2005) *The Psychology of the Language Learner: Individual Differences in Second Language Acquisition.* Mahwah, NJ: Lawrence Erlbaum. p. 91.

51 Corno, L. (1993). The best-laid plans: Modern conceptions of volition and educational re- search. *Educational Researcher,* 22, 14-22.

52 Weinstein, C.E., Husman, J. & Dierking, D.R. (2000). Self-regulation interventions with a focus on learning strategies. In M. Boekaerts, P.R. Pintrich, & M. Zeidner (Eds.), *Handbook of self-regulation* (pp. 728-748). San Diego, CA: Academic Press. Weinstein,

53 Winne, P.H. (1995). Inherent details in self-regulated learning. *Educational Psychologist,* 30, 173-187.

54 Zimmerman, B.J. (1998). Developing self-fulfilling cycles of academic regulation: An analysis of exemplary instructional model. In D.H. Schunk & B.J. Zimmerman (Eds.), *Self- regulated learning: From teaching to self-reflective practice* (pp. 1-19). New York: Guilford.

55 Zimmerman, B.J. (2000). Attaining self-regulation: A social cognitive perspective. In M. Boekaerts, P.R. Pintrich & M. Zeidner (Eds.), *Handbook of self-regulation* (pp. 451-502). San Diego, CA: Academic Press.

56 Zimmerman, B.J. (2001). Achieving academic excellence: A self-regulatory perspective. En M. Ferrari (Ed.), *The pursuit of excellence through education* (pp. 85-110). Mahwah, NJ: Erlbaum.

57 Zimmerman, B.J. (2002). Becoming a self-regulated learner: An overview. *Theory into Practice,* 41, 64-72.

58 Moffitt, T. E., Arseneault, L., Belsky, D., Dickson, N., Hancox, R. J., Harrington, H., Caspi, A. (2011). A gradient of childhood self-control predicts health, wealth, and public safety. *Proceedings of the National Academy of Sciences of the United States of America*, 108(7), 2693–8.

Printed in Great Britain
by Amazon